THE VOYAGE OF THE *PHAROS*

WALTER SCOTT'S CRUISE AROUND SCOTLAND IN 1814

WALTER SCOTT

Scottish Library Association
1998

The cover and text illustrations are from
aquatints and engravings by
William Daniell in
A voyage round Great Britain,
1818.
Courtesy Mitchell Library, Glasgow.

Introduction © Brian D Osborne

This edition © Scottish Library Association 1998.

ISBN 0 900649 46 1

Designed by **GSB**, Edinburgh

Scottish Library Association
Scottish Centre for Information & Library Services
1 John Street
Hamilton ML3 7EU

Printed by Antony Rowe Ltd.

The Voyage of the *Pharos*

―――――――◆―――――――

INTRODUCTION

―――――――◆―――――――

In the late summer of 1814 Walter Scott took advantage of the long court recess to sail round Scotland as a guest of the Commissioners of the Northern Lights, on their inspection cruise in the Lighthouse Yacht *Pharos*.

Scott was Sheriff-Depute of Selkirkshire and held an appointment as a Clerk of the Court of Session in Edinburgh. He was also a poet of national, and indeed international, reputation - the author of acclaimed works such as *Marmion* and *The Lady of the Lake*. His poetic reputation was so great that he had, in 1813, been offered the Poet Laureateship by the Prince Regent (later George IV). Scott had tactfully refused the offer, claiming that he held enough public appointments already, but, privately, not relishing the duty of composing poems to order for state occasions; he did however accept a Baronetcy in 1818. At the time of the lighthouse voyage, Scott was working on a long historical epic, *The Lord of the Isles*, and undoubtedly one attraction of the Commissioners' invitation was the opportunity to sail among the Hebrides and garner local colour for the work in hand.

Just three weeks before the *Pharos* sailed from Leith, the Edinburgh publishing house of Constable had issued a three volume novel - *Waverley; or 'tis sixty years since*. This groundbreaking historical novel set in the period of the 1745 Jacobite Rising sold out its first edition in five weeks and was greeted with enthusiastic reviews. *Waverley* was issued anonymously and for many years Scott officially denied authorship of it and its successors, probably because novel writing was thought a somewhat less respectable occupation for a senior legal figure than writing epic poetry or even folk-song collecting. The myth of "The Great Unknown" or "The Author of Waverley" grew up - but the reviewer in *The Scots Magazine* of July 1814 gave a pretty clear hint as to its authorship:

Report assigns it to the most admired poet of the age and we see no reason that even such a writer could have to disown a performance like the present.

Scott would be among far-distant islands and thus quite out of touch when the London reviews of *Waverley* appeared and his apparent ability to shut off that part of his life and concentrate on the experiences and adventures of the voyage is remarkable.

Scott resolved to keep a diary throughout his voyage and his five notebooks record in considerable detail the sights and experiences he and his companions enjoyed during their six week cruise. On board the *Pharos* were three fellow-Sheriffs who were, *ex officio*, Commissioners of the Northern Lights, and another two guests. However, despite the presence of the Commissioners and guests, Scott notes that:

the official chief of the expedition is Mr Stevenson, the Surveyor-Viceroy over the Commissioners - a most gentlemanlike and modest man, and well known by his scientific skill.

"Mr Stevenson" was Robert Stevenson, engineer to the Commissioners, designer of the Bell Rock Lighthouse, founder of the Stevenson dynasty of lighthouse engineers, and, of course, grandfather of another Scottish novelist, Robert Louis Stevenson.

The *Pharos's* route took Scott and his companions up the East Coast to Shetland, down to Orkney, through the Pentland Firth into the Minch and out to Harris, returning via Skye, the Small Isles, Mull and Iona, before crossing to Northern Ireland and returning to Greenock on the Clyde, where Scott took one of the newly introduced steamships upriver to Glasgow.

The expedition was not without its risks, quite apart from the ever-present dangers of the sea there was a very real threat from enemy ships. While Europe was at last at peace, with Napoleon confined on Elba, Britain was still at war with the United States. American privateers were taking prizes in Scottish waters and the *Pharos* narrowly avoided encounters with two such vessels in the waters between Islay and Ireland.

Scott's observations are not simply confined to landscape and the picturesque - he is also a perceptive observer of social conditions, agriculture and industry. Scott had an enquiring mind and his account of the economics and social impact of the Greenland whaling industry in Shetland demonstrates his concern for detail and indeed his fascination with exact information. Travelling through the Highlands and Islands during the early phase of the Highland Clearances, Scott has much to say about agricultural improvement and the need for change. However he reveals a sympathy and concern for all those caught up in what was an intractable problem of poor living standards, outmoded agricultural practices and rising population. In Shetland he wrote:

The proprietors are already upon the alert, studying the means of gradual improvement, and no humane person would wish them to drive it on too rapidly, to the distress and perhaps destruction of the numerous tenants who have been bred under a different system

As befitted a writer whose first major work had been *Minstrelsy of the Scottish Border*, Scott was a keen folklorist, and recorded tales of trolls in Shetland, visited a wind-seller in Orkney and recorded tales of clan feuds and massacres in the Hebrides. An assiduous antiquarian, Scott took in the classic sights in the Northern Isles, including the Broch of Mousa, the Dwarfie Stane, Scalloway Castle and St Magnus Cathedral and his experiences in Orkney and Shetland would be put to good use later in his 1822 novel *The Pirate*.

A highlight of the cruise was the visit to Skerryvore, fourteen miles off Tiree, where Stevenson planned to build a lighthouse in what was perhaps the most difficult oceanic environment yet attempted. Despite stormy weather Scott and his friends managed to land on this bare rock and:

took possession of the rock in the name of the Commissioners, and generously bestowed our own great names on its crags and rocks.

A shadow was cast over the final stage of the journey when Scott received word of the sudden death of Harriet, Duchess of Buccleuch. Scott was friendly with the Buccleuchs, regarding the Duke as the chief of his name and indeed had owed his appointment as Sheriff-Depute of Selkirk to the Duke's influence.

Scott's diary of his summer cruise reveals an informal, off-duty Scott, with a light touch and a great capacity for friendship and enjoyment. It is, indeed, a valuable document portraying the Highlands and Islands of Scotland at a period of significant change and social upheaval. It is an important work of travel and description, contributing to the discovery of Scotland by a wider audience - a process to which Scott's poetry and novels made a major contribution. However it is, above all, an enjoyable, entertaining and highly accessible account of an adventurous voyage in which, as he concludes, he had:

enjoyed as much pleasure as in any six weeks of my life. We had constant exertion, a succession of wild and uncommon scenery, good- humour on board, and objects of animation and interest when we went ashore .

All of which Scott communicates to his readers with a novelist's skill and a poet's grace.

Although some extracts from the diary were published by Scott in his lifetime the complete text was first published in 1837/38 by his son-in- law, John Gibson Lockhart, in his classic biography, *A Memoir of the Life of Sir Walter Scott*. The footnotes to the present edition are Lockhart's from the *Life*. Scott's spelling of place names often varies from modern convention, for example Zetland for Shetland, Loch Scavig for Loch Scavaig, Tyree for Tiree. However all are reasonably understandable and no attempt has been made to modernise Scott's text.

Brian D Osborne

The Port of Leith

VACATION 1814

---◆---

Voyage in the Lighthouse Yacht to Nova Zembla, and the Lord knows where.

July 29th, 1814. — Sailed from Leith about one o'clock on board the Lighthouse Yacht, conveying six guns, and ten men, commanded by Mr. Wilson. The company — Commissioners of the Northern Lights; Robert Hamilton, Sheriff of Lanarkshire; William Erskine, Sheriff of Orkney and Zetland; Adam Duff, Sheriff of Forfarshire. Non-Commissioners — Ipse Ego; Mr. David Marjoribanks, son to John Marjoribanks, Provost of Edinburgh, a young gentleman; Rev. Mr. Turnbull, minister of Tingwall, in the presbytery of Shetland. But the official chief of the expedition is Mr. Stevenson, the Surveyor-Viceroy over the Commissioners — a most gentlemanlike and modest man, and well known by his scientific skill.

Reached the Isle of May in the evening; went ashore, and saw the light — an old tower, and much in the form of a border-keep, with a beacon-grate on the top. It is to be abolished for an oil revolving-light, the gratefire only being ignited upon the leeward side when the wind is very high. *Quære* — Might not the grate revolve? The isle had once a cell or two upon it. The vestiges of the chapel are still visible. Mr. Stevenson proposed demolishing the old tower, and I recommended *ruining* it *à la picturesque* — *i.e.* demolishing it partially. The island might be made a delightful residence for sea-bathers.

On board again in the evening : watched the progress of the ship round Fifeness, and the revolving motion of the now distant Bell-Rock light until the wind grew rough, and the landsmen sick. To bed at eleven, and slept sound.

30th July. — Waked at six by the steward: summoned to visit the Bell-Rock, where the beacon is well worthy attention. Its dimensions are well known; but no description can give the idea of this slight, solitary, round tower, trembling amid the billows, and fifteen miles from Arbroath, the nearest shore. The fitting up within is not only handsome, but elegant. All work of wood (almost) is wainscot; all hammer-work brass; in short, exquisitely fitted up. You enter by a ladder of rope, with wooden steps, about thirty feet from the bottom, where the mason-work ceases to be solid, and admits of round apartments. The lowest is a storehouse for the people's provisions, water, etc.; above that a storehouse for the lights, of oil, etc. ; then the kitchen of the people, three in number; then their sleeping chamber; then the saloon or parlour, a neat little room; above all, the lighthouse; all communicating by oaken ladders, with brass rails, most handsomely and conveniently executed. Breakfasted in the parlour.[1] On board again at nine, and run down through a rough sea, to Aberbrothock, vulgarly called Arbroath. All sick, even Mr. Stevenson. God grant this occur seldom! Landed and dined at Arbroath, where we were to take up Adam Duff. We visited the appointments of the lighthouse establishment — a handsome tower, with two wings. These contain the lodgings of the keepers of the light — very handsome, indeed, and very clean. They might be thought too handsome were it not of consequence to give those men, intrusted with a duty so laborious and slavish, a consequence in the eyes of the public and in their own. The central part of the building forms a single tower, corresponding

---

[1]   On being requested, while at breakfast, to inscribe his name in the album of the tower, Scott penned immediately the following lines:-

PHAROS LOQUITUR.

Far in the bosom of the deep,
O'er these wild shelves my watch I keep;
A ruddy gem of changeful light,
Bound on the dusky brow of night,
The seaman bids my lustre hail,
And scorns to strike his timorous sail.

with the lighthouse. As the keepers' families live here, they are apprised each morning by a signal that *all is well*. If this signal be not made, a tender sails for the rock directly. I visited the abbey church for the third time, the first, being — eheu![1] — the second with T. Thomson. Dined at Arbroath, and came on board at night, where I made up this foolish journal, and now beg for wine and water. So the vessel is once more in motion.

31st July. — Waked at seven; vessel off Fowlsheugh and Dunnottar. Fair wind, and delightful day; glide enchantingly along the coast of Kincardineshire, and open the bay of Nigg about ten. At eleven, off Aberdeen; the gentlemen go ashore to Girdle-Ness, a projecting point of rock to the east of the harbour of Foot-Dee. There the magistrates of Aberdeen wish to have a fort and beacon-light. The Oscar, whaler, was lost here last year, with all her hands, excepting two; about forty perished. Dreadful, to be wrecked so near a large and populous town! The view of Old and New Aberdeen from the sea is quite beautiful. About noon, proceed along the coast of Aberdeenshire, which, to the northwards, changes from a bold and rocky to a low and sandy character. Along the bay of Belhelvie, a whole parish was swallowed up by the shifting sands, and is still a desolate waste. It belonged to the Earls of Errol, and was rented at £500 a year at the time. When these sands are past, the land is all arable. Not a tree to be seen; nor a grazing cow, or sheep, or even a labour-horse at grass, though this be Sunday. The next remarkable object was a fragment of the old castle of Slains, on a precipitous bank, overlooking the sea. The fortress was destroyed when James VI. marched north [A.D. 1594] after the battle of Glenlivat, to reduce Huntly and Errol to obedience. The family then removed to their present mean habitation, for such it seems, a collection of low houses forming a quadrangle, one side of which is built on the very verge of the precipice that overhangs the ocean. What seems odd, there are no stairs down to the beach. Imprudence, or ill fortune as fatal as the sands of Belhelvie, has swallowed up the estate of Errol, excepting this dreary mansion-house, and a farm or two adjoining. We took to the boat, and running along the coast, had some delightful sea-views to the northward of the castle. The coast is here

---

[1] This is, without doubt, an allusion to some happy day's excursion when his *first love* was of the party.

Slanes Castle, Aberdeenshire

very rocky; but the rocks, being rather soft, are wasted and corroded by the constant action of the waves, — and the fragments which remain, where the softer parts have been washed away, assume the appearance of old Gothic ruins. There are open arches, towers, steeples, and so forth. One part of this scaur is called *Dun Buy*, being coloured yellow by the dung of the sea-fowls, who build there in the most surprising numbers. We caught three young gulls. But the most curious object was the celebrated Buller of Buchan, a huge rocky cauldron, into which the sea rushes through a natural arch of rock. I walked round the top; in one place the path is only about two feet wide, and a monstrous precipice on either side. We then rowed into the cauldron or buller from beneath, and saw nothing around us but a regular wall of black rock, and nothing above but the blue sky. A fishing hamlet had sent out its inhabitants, who gazing from the brink, looked like sylphs looking down upon gnomes. In the side of the cauldron opens a deep black cavern. Johnson says it might be a retreat from storms, which is nonsense. In a high gale the waves rush in with incredible violence. An old fisher said he had seen them flying over the natural wall of the buller, which cannot be less than 200 feet high. Same old man says, Slains is now inhabited by a Mr. Bowles, who comes so far from the southward that naebody kens whare he comes frae. "Was he frae the Indies?" — "Na; he did not think he came that road. He was far frae the southland. Naebody ever heard the name of the place ; but he had brought more guid out o' Peterhead than a' the Lords he had seen in Slains, and he had seen three." About half past five we left this interesting spot, and after a hard pull, reached the yacht. Weather falls hazy, and rather calm; but at sea we observe vessels enjoying more wind. Pass Peterhead, dimly distinguishing two steeples, and a good many masts. Mormounthill said to resemble a coffin — a likeness of which we could not judge, Mormount being for the present invisible. Pass Rattray-Head: near this cape are dangerous shelves, called the Bridge of Rattray. Here the wreck of the Doris merchant vessel came on shore, lost last year with a number of passengers for Shetland. We lie off all night.

1st August. — Off Fraserburgh — a neat little town. Mr. Stevenson and the Commissioners go on shore to look at a light maintained there upon an old castle, on a cape called Kinnaird's Head. The morning being rainy, and no object of curiosity ashore, I remain on board, to make up my journal, and write home.

The old castle, now bearing the light, is a picturesque object from the sea. It was the baronial mansion of the Frasers, now Lords Saltoun — an old square tower with a minor fortification towards the landing-place on the sea-side. About eleven, the Commissioners came off, and we leave this town, the extreme point of the Moray Firth, to stretch for Shetland — salute the castle with three guns, and stretch out with a merry gale. See Mormount, a long flattish-topped hill near to the West Trouphead, and another bold cliff promontory projecting into the firth. Our gale soon failed, and we are now all but becalmed; songs, ballads, recitations, backgammon, and piquet, for the rest of the day. Noble sunset and moon rising; we are now out of sight of land.

2nd August. — At sea in the mouth of the Moray Firth. This day almost a blank–light baffling airs, which do us very little good; most of the landsmen sick, more or less; piquet, backgammon, and chess, the only resources. — *P.M.* A breeze, and we begin to think we have passed the Fair Isle, lying between Shetland and Orkney, at which it was our intention to have touched. In short, like one of Sinbad's adventures, we have run on till neither captain nor pilot know exactly where we are. The breeze increases — weather may be called rough; worse and worse after we are in our berths, nothing but booming, trampling, and whizzing of waves about our ears, and ever and anon, as we fall asleep, our ribs come in contact with those of the vessel; hail Duff and the Udaller[1] in the after-cabin, but they are too sick to answer. Towards morning, calm (comparative), and a nap.

3rd August. — At sea as before; no appearance of land; proposed that the Sheriff of Zetland do issue a *meditatione fugæ* warrant against his territories, which seem to fly from us. Pass two whalers; speak the nearest, who had come out of Lerwick, which is about twenty miles distant; stand on with a fine breeze. About nine at night, with moonlight and strong twilight, we weather the point of Bardhead, and enter a channel about three quarters of a mile broad, which forms the southern entrance to the harbour of Lerwick, where we cast anchor about half-past ten, and put Mr. Turnbull on shore.

---

[1]   Erskine - Sheriff of Shetland and Orkney.

4th August. — Harbour of Lerwick. Admire the excellence of this harbour of the metropolis of Shetland. It is a most beautiful place, screened on all sides from the wind by hills of a gentle elevation. The town, a fishing village built irregularly upon a hill ascending from the shore, has a picturesque appearance. On the left is Fort Charlotte, garrisoned of late by two companies of veterans. The Greenlandmen, of which nine fine vessels are lying in the harbour, add much to the liveliness of the scene. Mr. Duncan, sheriff-substitute, came off to pay his respects to his principal; he is married to a daughter of my early acquaintance, Walter Scott of Scotshall. We go ashore. Lerwick, a poor-looking place, the streets flagged instead of being causewayed, for there are no wheel-carriages. The streets full of drunken riotous sailors, from the whale-vessels. It seems these ships take about 1000 sailors from Zetland every year, and return them as they come back from the fishery. Each sailor may gain from £20 to £30, which is paid by the merchants of Lerwick, who have agencies from the owners of the whalers in England. The whole return may be between £25,000 and £30,000. These Zetlanders, as they get a part of this pay on landing, make a point of treating their English messmates, who get drunk of course, and are very riotous. The Zetlanders themselves do *not* get drunk, but go straight home to their houses, and reserve their hilarity for the winter season, when they spend their wages in dancing and drinking. Erskine finds employment as Sheriff, for the neighbourhood of the fort enables him to make *main forte*, and secure a number of the rioters. We visit F. Charlotte, which is a neat little fort mounting ten heavy guns to the sea, but only one to the land. Major F., the Governor, showed us the fort; it commands both entrances of the harbour: the north entrance is not very good, but the south capital. The water in the harbour is very deep, as frigates of the smaller class lie almost close to the shore. Take a walk with Captain M'Diarmid, a gentlemanlike and intelligent officer of the garrison; we visit a small fresh-water loch called *Cleik-him-in*; it borders on the sea, from which it is only divided by a sort of beach, apparently artificial: though the sea lashes the outside of this beach, the water of the lake is not brackish. In this lake are the remains of a Picts' Castle, but ruinous. The people think the Castle has not been built on a natural island, but on an artificial one formed by a heap of stones. These Duns or Picts' Castles are so small, it is impossible to conceive what effectual purpose they could serve excepting a temporary refuge for the chief. — Leave *Cleik-him-in*, and proceed along the coast. The ground is dreadfully encumbered with stones; the *patches* which have been sown with oats and barley, bear very good crops, but they are mere patches, the cattle and ponies feeding amongst them, and secured by tethers. The houses most wretched, worse than the worst herd's house I ever saw. It would be easy to form a good farm by enclosing the ground with Galloway dykes, which would answer the purpose of clearing it at the same time of stones; and as there is plenty of lime-shell, marle, and alga-marina, manure could not be wanting. But there are several obstacles to improvement, chiefly the undivided state of the properties, which lie *run-rig*; then the claims of Lord Dundas, the lord of the country, and above all, perhaps, the state of the common people, who, dividing their attention between the fishery and the cultivation, are not much interested in the latter, and are often absent at the proper times of labour. Their ground is chiefly dug with the spade, and their ploughs are beyond description awkward. An odd custom prevails — any person, without exception (if I understand rightly), who wishes to raise a few kail, fixes upon any spot he pleases, encloses it with a dry stone wall, uses it as a kail-yard till he works out the soil, then deserts it and makes another. Some dozen of these little enclosures, about twenty or thirty feet square, are in sight at once. They are called *planty-cruives*; and the Zetlanders are so far from reckoning this an invasion, or a favour on the part of the proprietor, that their most exaggerated description of an avaricious person is one who would refuse liberty for a *planty-cruive*; or to infer the greatest contempt of another, they will say, they would not hold a *planty-cruive* of him. It is needless to notice how much this licence must interfere with cultivation.

Leaving the *cultivated* land, we turn more inland, and pass two or three small lakes. The muirs are mossy and sterile in the highest degree; the hills are clad with stunted heather, intermixed with huge great stones; much of an astringent root with a yellow flower, called *Tormentil*, used by the islanders in dressing leather in lieu of the oak bark. We climbed a hill, about three miles from Lerwick, to a cairn which presents a fine view of the indented coast of the island, and the distant isles of Mousa and others. Unfortunately the day is rather hazy— return by a circuitous route, through the same sterile country.

These muirs are used as a commonty by the proprietors of the parishes in which they lie, and each, without any regard to the extent of his peculiar property, puts as much stock upon them as he chooses. The sheep are miserable-looking, hairy-legged creatures, of all colours, even to sky-blue. I often wondered where Jacob got speckled lambs; I think now they must have been of the Shetland stock. In our return, pass the upper end of the little lake of *Cleik-him-in*, which is divided by a rude causeway from another small loch, communicating with it, however, by a sluice, for the purpose of driving a mill. But such a mill! The wheel is horizontal, with the cogs turned diagonally to the water; the beam stands upright, and is inserted in a stone-quern of the old-fashioned construction. This simple machine is enclosed in a hovel about the size of a pig-stye -and there is the mill![1] There are about 500 such mills in Shetland, each incapable of grinding more than a sack at a time.

I cannot get a distinct account of the nature of the land rights. The Udal proprietors have ceased to exist, yet proper feudal tenures seem ill understood. Districts of ground are in many instances understood to belong to Townships or Communities, possessing what may be arable by patches, and what is muir as a commonty, *pro indiviso*. But then individuals of such a Township often take it upon them to grant feus of particular parts of the property thus possessed *pro indiviso*. The town of Lerwick is built upon a part of the commonty of Sound, the proprietors of the houses having feu-rights from different heritors of that Township, but why from one rather than another, or how even the whole Township combining (which has not yet been attempted) could grant such a right upon principle, seems altogether uncertain. In the meantime the chief stress is laid upon occupance. I should have supposed, upon principle, that Lord Dundas, as superior, possessed the *dominium eminens*, and ought to be resorted to as the source of land rights. But it is not so. It has been found that the heritors of each Township hold directly of the Crown, only paying the *Scat*, or Norwegian land-tax, and other duties to his lordship, used and wont. Besides, he has what are called property lands in every Township, or in most, which he lets to his tenants. Lord Dundas is now trying to

---

[1]   Here occurs a rude scratch of drawing.

introduce the system of leases and a better kind of agriculture.[1] Return home and dine at Sinclair's, a decent inn — Captain M'Diarmid and other gentlemen dine with us. — Sleep at the inn on a straw couch.

5th August, 1814. — Hazy disagreeable morning; — Erskine trying the rioters — notwithstanding which, a great deal of rioting still in the town. The Greenlanders, however, only quarrelled among themselves, and the Zetland sailors seemed to exert themselves in keeping peace. They are, like all the other Zetlanders I have seen, a strong, clear-complexioned, handsome race, and the women are very pretty. The females are rather slavishly employed, however, and I saw more than one carrying home the heavy sea-chests of their husbands, brothers, or lovers, discharged from on board the Greenlanders. The Zetlanders are, however, so far provident, that when they enter the navy they make liberal allowance of their pay for their wives and families. Not less than £15,000 a year has been lately paid by the Admiralty on this account; yet this influx of money, with that from the Greenland fishery, seems rather to give the means of procuring useless indulgences than of augmenting the stock of productive labour. Mr. Collector Ross tells me that from the King's books it appears that the quantity of spirits, tea, coffee, tobacco, snuff, and sugar imported annually into Lerwick for the consumption of Zetland averages at sale price £20,000 yearly at the least. Now the inhabitants of Zetland, men, women, and children, do not exceed 22,000 in all, and the proportion of foreign luxuries seems monstrous, unless we allow for the habits contracted by the seamen in their foreign trips. Tea, in particular, is used by all ranks, and porridge quite exploded.

We parade Lerwick. The most remarkable thing is, that the main street being flagged, and all the others very narrow lanes descending the hill by steps, anything like a cart, of the most ordinary and rude construction, seems not only out of question when the town was built, but in its present state quite excluded. A road of five miles in length, on the line between Lerwick and Scalloway, has been already made — upon a very awkward and expensive plan, and ill-lined as may be supposed. But it is proposed to extend this road by degrees: carts will then be introduced, and by crossing the breed of their ponies

---

[1]   Lord Dundas was created Earl of Zetland in 1838, and died in February 1839.

judiciously, they will have Galloways to draw them. The streets of Lerwick (as one blunder perpetrates another) will then be a bar to improvement, for till the present houses are greatly altered, no cart can approach the quay. In the garden of Captain Nicolson, R.N., which is rather in a flourishing state, he has tried various trees, almost all of which have died except the willow. But the plants seem to me to be injured in their passage; seeds would perhaps do better. We are visited by several of the notables of the island, particularly Mr. Mowat, a considerable proprietor, who claims acquaintance with me as the friend of my father and remembers me as a boy. The day clearing up, Duff and I walk with this good old gentleman to *Cleik-him-in*, and with some trouble drag a boat off the beach into the fresh-water loch, and go to visit the Picts' castle. It is of considerable size, and consists of three circular walls, of huge natural stones admirably combined without cement. The outer circuit seems to have been simply a bounding wall or bulwark; the second or interior defence contains lodgements such as I shall describe. This inner circuit is surrounded by a wall of about sixteen or eighteen feet thick, composed, as I said, of huge massive stones placed in layers with great art, but without mortar or cement. The wall is not perpendicular, but the circle lessens gradually towards the top, as an old-fashioned pigeon-house. Up the interior of this wall there proceeds a circular winding gallery ascending in the form of an inclined plane, so as to gain the top by circling round like a cork-screw within the walls. This is enlightened by little apertures (about two feet by three) into the inside, and also, it is said, by small slits — of which I saw none. It is said there are marks of galleries within the circuit, running parallel to the horizon; these I saw no remains of; and the interior gallery, with its apertures, is so extremely low and narrow, being only about three feet square, that it is difficult to conceive how it could serve the purpose of communication. At any rate, the size fully justifies the tradition prevalent here as well as in the south of Scotland, that the Picts were a diminutive race. More of this when we see the more perfect specimen of a Pict castle in Mousa, which we resolve to examine, if it be possible. Certainly I am deeply curious to see what must be one of the most ancient houses in the world, built by a people who, while they seem to have bestowed much pains on their habitations, knew neither the art of cement, of arches, or of stairs. The situation is wild, dreary, and impressive. On the land side are huge sheets and fragments of rocks, interspersed with a stinted vegetation of grass and heath, which bears no proportion to the rocks and stones. From the top of his tower the Pictish Monarch might look out upon a stormy sea, washing a succession of rocky capes, reaches, and headlands, and immediately around him was the deep fresh-water loch on which his fortress was constructed. It communicates with the land by a sort of causeway, formed, like the artificial islet itself, by heaping together stones till the pile reached the surface of the water. This is usually passable, but at present over-flooded. — Return and dine with Mr. Duncan, Sheriff-Substitute — are introduced to Dr. Edmonstone, author of a History of Shetland, who proposes to accompany us to-morrow to see the Cradle of Noss. I should have mentioned that Mr. Stevenson sailed this morning with the yacht to survey some isles to the northward; he returns on Saturday, it is hoped.

6th August. — Hire a six-oared boat, whaler-built, with a taper point at each end, so that the rudder can be hooked on either at pleasure. These vessels look very frail, but are admirably adapted to the stormy seas, where they live when a ship's boat stiffly and compactly built must necessarily perish. They owe this to their elasticity and lightness. Some of the rowers wear a sort of coats of dressed sheep leather, sewed together with thongs. We sailed out at the southern inlet of the harbour, rounding successively the capes of the Hammer, Kirkubus, the Ving, and others, consisting of bold cliffs, hollowed into caverns, or divided into pillars and arches of fantastic appearance, by the constant action of the waves. As we passed the most northerly of these capes, called, I think, the Ord, and turned into the open sea, the scenes became yet more tremendously sublime. Rocks upwards of three or four hundred feet in height, presented themselves in gigantic succession, sinking perpendicularly into the main, which is very deep even within a few fathoms of their base. One of these capes is called the Bard-head; a huge projecting arch is named the Giant's Leg.

> *Here the lone sea-bird wakes its wildest cry.*[1]

Not lone, however, in one sense, for their numbers and the variety of their tribes are immense, though I think they do not quite equal

[1]   Campbell - *Pleasures of Hope.*

those of Dunbuy, on the coast of Buchan. Standing across a little bay, we reached the Isle of Noss, having hitherto coasted the shore of Bressay. Here we see a detached and precipitous rock, or island, being a portion rent by a narrow sound from the rest of the cliff, and called the Holm. This detached rock is wholly inaccessible, unless by a pass of peril, entitled the Cradle of Noss, which is a sort of wooden chair, travelling from precipice to precipice on rings, which run upon two cables stretched across over the gulf. We viewed this extraordinary contrivance from beneath, at the distance of perhaps one hundred fathoms at least. The boatmen made light of the risk of crossing it, but it must be tremendous to a brain disposed to be giddy. Seen from beneath, a man in the basket would resemble a large crow or raven floating between rock and rock. The purpose of this strange contrivance is to give the tenant the benefit of putting a few sheep upon the Holm, the top of which is level, and affords good pasture. The animals are transported in the cradle by one at a time, a shepherd holding them upon his knees. The channel between the Holm and the isle is passable by boats in calm weather, but not at the time when we saw it. Rowing on through a heavy tide, and nearer the breakers than any but Zetlanders would have ventured, we rounded another immensely high cape, called by the islanders the Noup of Noss, but by sailors Hang-cliff, from its having a projecting appearance. This was the highest rock we had yet seen, though not quite perpendicular. Its height has never been measured: I should judge it exceeds 600 feet; it has been conjectured to measure 800 and upwards. Our steersman had often descended this precipitous rock, having only the occasional assistance of a rope, one end of which he secured from time to time round some projecting cliff. The collecting sea-fowl for their feathers was the object, and he might gain five or six dozen, worth eight or ten shillings, by such an adventure. These huge precipices abound with caverns, many of which run much farther into the rock than any one has ventured to explore. We entered (with much hazard to our boat) one called the Orkney-man's Harbour, because an Orkney vessel run in there some years since to escape a French privateer. The entrance was lofty enough to admit us without striking the mast, but a sudden turn in the direction of the cave would have consigned us to utter darkness if we had gone in farther. The dropping of the sea-fowl and cormorants into the water from the sides of the cavern, when disturbed by our approach, had something in it wild and terrible.

After passing the Noup, the precipices become lower, and sink into a rocky shore with deep indentations, called by the natives *Gios*. Here we would fain have landed to visit the Cradle from the top of the cliff, but the surf rendered it impossible. We therefore rowed on like Thalaba in "Allah's name," around the Isle of Noss, and landed upon the opposite side of the small sound which divides it from Bressay. Noss exactly resembles in shape Salisbury crags, supposing the sea to flow down the valley called the Hunter's bog, and round the foot of the precipice. The eastern part of the isle is fine smooth pasture, the best I have seen in these isles, sloping upwards to the verge of the tremendous rocks which form its western front.

As we are to dine at Gardie-House (the seat of young Mr. Mowat), on the Isle of Bressay, Duff and I — who went together on this occasion — resolve to walk across the island, about three miles, being by this time thoroughly wet. Bressay is a black and heathy isle, full of little lochs and bogs. Through storm and shade, and dense and dry, we find our way to Gardie, and have then to encounter the sublunary difficulties of wanting the keys of our portmanteaus, etc., the servants having absconded to see the Cradle. These being overcome, we are most hospitably treated at Gardie. Young Mr. Mowat, son of my old friend, is an improver, and a *moderate* one. He has got a ploughman from Scotland, who acts as *grieve*, but as yet with the prejudices and inconveniences which usually attach themselves to the most salutary experiments. The ploughman complains that the Zetlanders work as if a spade or hoe burned their fingers, and that though they only got a shilling a day, yet the labour of three of them does not exceed what one good hand in Berwickshire would do for 2s.6d. The islanders retort, that a man can do no more than he can; that they are not used to be taxed to their work so severely; that they will work as their fathers did, and not otherwise; and at first the landlord found difficulty in getting hands to work under his Caledonian taskmaster. Besides, they find fault with his *ho*, and *gee*, and *wo*, when ploughing. "He speaks to the horse," they say, " and they gang — and there's something no canny about the man." In short, between the prejudices of laziness and superstition, the ploughman leads a sorry life of it; yet these prejudices are daily abating, under the steady and indulgent management of the proprietor. Indeed, nowhere is improvement in agriculture more necessary. An old-fashioned Zetland plough is a real curiosity. It had but one handle, or stilt, and a coulter, but no sock; it ripped the furrow, therefore, but did not throw it aside. When this precious machine was in motion, it was dragged by four little bullocks yoked abreast, and as many ponies harnessed, or rather strung, to the plough by ropes and thongs of raw hide. One man went before walking backward, with his face to the bullocks, and pulling them forward by main strength. Another held down the plough by its single handle, and made a sort of slit in the earth, which two women, who closed the procession, converted into a furrow, by throwing the earth aside with shovels. An antiquary might be of opinion that this was the very model of the original plough invented by Triptolemus; and it is but justice to Zetland to say that these relics of ancient agricultural art will soon have all the interest attached to rarity. We could only hear of one of these ploughs within three miles of Lerwick.

This and many other barbarous habits to which the Zetlanders were formerly wedded, seem only to have subsisted because their amphibious character of fishers and farmers induced them to neglect agricultural arts. A Zetland farmer looks to the sea to pay his rent; if the land finds him a little meal and kail, and (if he be a very clever fellow) a few potatoes, it is very well. The more intelligent part of the landholders are sensible of all this, but argue like men of good sense and humanity on the subject. To have good farming, you must have a considerable farm, upon which capital may be laid out to advantage. But to introduce this change suddenly would turn adrift perhaps twenty families, who now occupy small farms *pro indiviso*, cultivating by patches, or *rundale* and *runrig*, what part of the property is arable, and stocking the pasture as a common upon which each family turns out such stock as they can rear, without observing any proportion as to the number which it can support. In this way many townships, as they are called, subsist indeed, but in a precarious and indigent manner. Fishing villages seem the natural resource for this excess of population; but, besides the expense of erecting them, the habits of the people are to be considered, who, with "one foot on land and one on sea," would be with equal reluctance confined to either element. The remedy seems to be, that the larger proprietors should gradually set the example of better cultivation, and introduce better implements. They will, by degrees, be imitated by the inferior proprietors, and by their tenants; and, as turnips and hay crops become more general, a better and heavier class of stock will naturally be introduced.

The sheep in particular might be improved into a valuable stock, and would no doubt thrive, since the winters are very temperate. But I should be sorry that extensive pasture farms were introduced, as it would tend to diminish a population invaluable for the supply of our navy. The improvement of the arable land, on the contrary, would soon set them beyond the terrors of famine with which the islanders are at present occasionally visited; and, combined with fisheries, carried on not by farmers but by real fishers, would amply supply the inhabitants, without diminishing the export of dried fish. This separation of trades will in time take place, and then the prosperous days of Zetland will begin. The proprietors are already upon the alert, studying the means of gradual improvement, and no humane person would wish them to drive it on too rapidly, to the distress and perhaps destruction of the numerous tenants who have been bred under a different system.

I have gleaned something of the peculiar superstitions of the Zetlanders, which are numerous and potent. Witches, fairies, etc., are as numerous as ever they were in Teviotdale. The latter are called *Trows*, probably from the Norwegian *Dwärg* (or *dwarf*) the D being readily converted into T. The dwarfs are the prime agents in the machinery of Norwegian superstition. The *trows* do not differ from the fairies of the Lowlands, or *Sighean* of the Highlanders. They steal children, dwell within the interior of green hills, and often carry mortals into their recesses. Some, yet alive, pretend to have been carried off in this way, and obtain credit for the marvels they tell of the subterranean habitations of the trows. Sometimes, when a person becomes melancholy and lowspirited, the trows are supposed to have stolen the real being, and left a moving phantom to represent him. Sometimes they are said to steal only the heart — like Lancashire witches. There are cures in each case. The party's friends resort to a cunning man or woman, who hangs about the neck a triangular stone in the shape of a heart, or conjures back the lost individual, by retiring to the hills and employing the necessary spells. A common receipt, when a child appears consumptive and puny, is, that the conjurer places a bowl of water on the patient's head, and pours melted lead into it through the wards of a key. The metal assumes of course a variety of shapes, from which he selects a portion, after due consideration, which is sewn into the shirt of the patient. Sometimes no part of the lead suits the seer's fancy. Then the operation is recommenced, until he obtains a fragment of such a configuration as suits his mystical purpose. Mr. Duncan told us he had been treated in this way when a boy.

A worse and most horrid opinion prevails, or did prevail, among the fishers — namely, that he who saves a drowning man will receive at his hands some deep wrong or injury. Several instances were quoted to-day in company, in which the utmost violence had been found necessary to compel the fishers to violate this inhuman prejudice. It is conjectured to have arisen as an apology for rendering no assistance to the mariners as they escaped from a shipwrecked vessel, for these isles are infamous for plundering wrecks. A story is told of the crew of a stranded vessel who were warping themselves ashore by means of a hawser which they had fixed to the land. The islanders (of Unst, as I believe) watched their motions in silence, till an old man reminded them that if they suffered these sailors to come ashore, they would consume all their winter stock of provisions. A Zetlander cut the hawser, and the poor wretches, twenty in number, were all swept away. This is a tale of former times — the cruelty would not now be *active*; but I fear that even yet the drowning mariner would in some places receive no assistance in his exertions, and certainly he would in most be plundered to the skin upon his landing. The gentlemen do their utmost to prevent this infamous practice. It may seem strange that the natives should be so little affected by a distress to which they are themselves so constantly exposed. But habitual exposure to danger hardens the heart against its consequences, whether to ourselves or others. There is yet living a man — if he can be called so — to whom the following story belongs: — He was engaged in catching sea-fowl upon one of the cliffs, with his father and brother. All three were suspended by a cord, according to custom, and overhanging the ocean at the height of some hundred feet. This man being uppermost on the cord, observed that it was giving way, as unable to support their united weight. He called out to his brother who was next to him — "Cut away a nail below, Willie," meaning he should cut the rope beneath, and let his father drop. Willie refused, and bid him cut himself, if he pleased. He did so, and his brother and father were precipitated into the sea. He never thought of concealing or denying the adventure in all its parts. We left Gardie House late; being on the side of the Isle of Bressay, opposite to Lerwick, we were soon rowed across the bay. A laugh with Hamilton,[1] whose gout keeps him stationary at Lerwick, but whose good-humour defies gout and every other provocation, concludes the evening.

7th August, 1814. — Being Sunday, Duff, Erskine, and I rode to Tingwall upon Zetland ponies, to breakfast with our friend Parson Turnbull, who had come over in our yacht. An ill-conducted and worse-made road served us four miles on our journey. This *Via Flaminia* of Thule terminates, like its prototype, in a bog. It is, however, the only road in these isles, except about half a mile made by Mr. Turnbull. The land in the interior much resembles the Peel-heights, near Ashestiel; but, as you approach the other side of the island, becomes better. Tingwall is rather a fertile valley, up which winds a loch of about two miles in length. The kirk and manse stand at the head of the loch, and command a view down the valley to another lake beyond the first, and thence over another reach of land, to the ocean, indented by capes and studded with isles; among which, that of St. Ninian's, abruptly divided from the mainland by a deep chasm, is the most conspicuous. Mr. Turnbull is a Jedburgh man by birth, but a Zetlander by settlement and inclination. I have reason to be proud of my countryman; — he is doing his best, with great patience and judgment, to set a good example both in temporals and spirituals, and generally beloved and respected among all classes. His glebe is in far the best order of any ground I have seen, in Zetland. It is enclosed

[1]   Robert Hamilton, Sheriff of Lanarkshire, and afterwards one of the Clerks of Session, was a particular favourite of Scott - first, among many other good reasons, because he had been a soldier in his youth, had fought gallantly and been wounded severely in the American war, and was a very Uncle Toby in military enthusiasm; 2ndly, because he was a brother antiquary of the genuine Monkbarns breed; 3rdly (last not least), because he was, in spite of the example of the head of his name and race, a steady Tory. Mr. Hamilton sent for Scott when upon his deathbed in 1831, and desired him to choose and carry off as a parting memorial any article he liked in his collection of arms. Sir Walter (by that time sorely shattered in his own health) selected the sword with which his good friend had been begirt at Bunker's Hill.

chiefly with dry-stone, instead of the useless turf-dykes; and he has sown grass, and has a hay-stack, and a second crop of clover, and may claim well-dressed fields of potatoes, barley, and oats. The people around him are obviously affected by his example. He gave us an excellent discourse and remarkably good prayers, which are seldom the excellence of the Presbyterian worship.[1] The congregation were numerous, decent, clean, and well-dressed. The men have all the air of seamen, and are a good-looking hardy race. Some of the old fellows had got faces much resembling Tritons; if they had had conchs to blow, it would have completed them. After church, ride down the loch to Scalloway — the country wild but pleasant, with sloping hills of good pasturage,and patches of cultivation on the lower ground. Pass a huge standing stone or pillar. Here, it is said, the son of an old Earl of the Orkneys met his fate. He had rebelled against his father, and fortified himself in Zetland. The Earl sent a party to dislodge him, who, not caring to proceed to violence against his person, failed in the attempt. The Earl then sent a stronger force, with orders to take him dead or alive. The young Absalom's castle was stormed — he himself fled across the loch, and was overtaken and slain at this pillar. The Earl afterwards executed the perpetrators of this slaughter, though they had only fulfilled his own mandate.

We reach Scalloway, and visit the ruins of an old castle, composed of a double tower or keep, with turrets at the corners. It is the principal if not the only ruin of Gothic times in Zetland, and is of very recent date, being built in 1600. It was built by Patrick Stewart, Earl of Orkney, afterwards deservedly executed at Edinburgh for many acts of tyranny and oppression. It was this rapacious Lord who imposed many of those heavy duties still levied from the Zetlanders by Lord Dundas. The exactions by which he accomplished this erection were represented as grievous. He was so dreaded, that upon his trial one Zetland witness refused to say a word till he was assured that there was no chance of the Earl returning to Scalloway. Over the entrance of the castle are his arms, much defaced, with the unicorns of Scotland for supporters, the assumption of which was one of the articles of

---

[1]   During the winter of 1837-8 this worthy clergyman's wife, his daughter, and a servant perished within sight of the manse, from a flaw in the ice on the loch - which they were crossing as the nearest way home. - [1839]

indictment. There is a Scriptural inscription also above the door, in Latin, now much defaced—

PATRICIUS ORCHADIÆ ET ZETLANDIÆ COMES.
A.D.1600. CUJUS FUNDAMEN SAXUM EST, DOMUS ILLA
MANEBIT STABILIS: E CONTRA, SI SIT ARENA, PERIT.

This is said to have been furnished to Earl Patrick by a Presbyterian divine, who slily couched under it an allusion to the evil practices by which the Earl had established his power. He perhaps trusted that the language might disguise the import from the Earl.[1] If so, the Scottish nobility are improved in literature, for the Duke of Gordon pointed out an error in the Latinity.

Scalloway has a beautiful and very safe harbour, but as it is somewhat difficult of access, from a complication of small islands, it is inferior to Lerwick. Hence, though still nominally the capital of Zetland, for all edictal citations are made at Scalloway, it has sunk into a small fishing hamlet. The Norwegians made their original settlement in this parish of Tingwall. At the head of this loch, and just below the manse, is a small round islet accessible by stepping stones, where they held their courts; hence the islet is called Law-ting — Ting, or Thing, answering to our word business, exactly like the Latin *negotium*. It seems odd that in Dumfriesshire, and even in the Isle of Man, where the race and laws were surely Celtic, we have this Gothic word Ting and Tingwald applied in the same way. We dined with Mr. Scott of Scalloway, who, like several families of this name in Shetland, is derived from the house of Scotstarvet. They are very clannish, marry much among themselves, and are proud of their descent. Two young

---

[1] In his reviewal of Pitcairn's Trials (1831), Scott says - 'In erecting this Earl's Castle of Scalloway, and other expensive edifices, the King's tenants were forced to work in quarries, transport stone, dig, delve, climb, and build, and submit to all possible sorts of servile and painful labour, without either meat, drink, hire, or recompense of any kind. "My father," said Earl Patrick, " built his house at Sumburgh on the sand, and it has given way already; this of mine on the rock shall abide and endure." He did not or would not understand that the oppression, rapacity and cruelty by means of which the house arose, were what the clergyman really pointed to in his recommendation of a motto. Accordingly, the huge tower remains wild and desolate - its chambers filled with sand, and its rifted walls and dismantled battlements giving unrestrained access to the roaring sea blast.

- For more of Earl Patrick, see Scott's Miscellaneous Prose Works, vol. xxi. pp.230, 233; vol. xxiii. pp. 327,329.

ladies, daughters of Mr. Scott's, dined with us — they were both Mrs. Scotts, having married brothers — the husband of one was lost in the unfortunate Doris. They were pleasant, intelligent women, and exceedingly obliging. Old Mr. Scott seems a good country gentleman. He is negotiating an exchange with Lord Dundas, which will give him the Castle of Scalloway and two or three neighbouring islands: the rest of the archipelago (seven, I think, in number) are already his own. He will thus have command of the whole fishing and harbour, for which he parts with an estate of more immediate value, lying on the other side of the mainland. I found my name made me very popular in this family, and there were many enquiries after the state of the Buccleuch family, in which they seemed to take much interest. I found them possessed of the remarkable circumstances attending the late projected sale of Ancrum, and the death of Sir John Scott, and thought it strange that, settled for three generations in a country so distant, they should still take an interest in those matters. I was loaded with shells and little curiosities for my young people.

There was a report (January was two years) of a kraken or some monstrous fish being seen off Scalloway. The object was visible for a fortnight, but nobody dared approach it, although I should have thought the Zetlanders would not have feared the devil if he came by water. They pretended that the suction, when they came within a certain distance, was so great as to endanger their boats. The object was described as resembling a vessel with her keel turned upmost in the sea, or a small ridge of rock or island. Mr. Scott thinks it might have been a vessel overset, or a large whale: if the latter, it seems odd they should not have known it, as whales are the intimate acquaintances of all Zetland sailors. Whatever it was, it disappeared after a heavy gale of wind, which seems to favour the idea that it was the wreck of a vessel. Mr. Scott seems to think Pontopiddan's narrations and descriptions are much more accurate than we inland men suppose; and I find most Zetlanders of the same opinion. Mr. Turnbull, who is not credulous upon these subjects, tells me that this year a parishioner of his, a well-informed and veracious person, saw an animal, which, if his description was correct, must have been of the species of sea-snake, driven ashore on one of the Orkneys two or three years ago. It was very long, and seemed about the thickness of a Norway log, and swam on the top of the waves, occasionally lifting and bending its head. Mr. T. says he has no doubt of the veracity of the narrator, but still thinks it possible it may have been a mere log or beam of wood, and that the spectator may have been deceived by the motion of the waves, joined to the force of imagination. This for the Duke of Buccleuch.

At Scalloway my curiosity was gratified by an account of the sword-dance, now almost lost, but still practised in the Island of Papa, belonging to Mr. Scott. There are eight performers, seven of whom represent the Seven Champions of Christendom, who enter one by one with their swords drawn, and are presented to the eighth personage, who is not named. Some rude couplets are spoken in *English*, not *Norse*), containing a sort of panegyric upon each champion as he is presented. They then dance a sort of cotillion, as the ladies described it, going through a number of evolutions with their swords. One of three Mrs. Scotts readily promised to procure me lines, the rhymes, and the form of the dance. I regret much that young Mr. Scott was absent during this visit; he is described as a reader and an enthusiast in poetry; Probably I might have interested him in preserving dance, by causing young persons to learn it. A few years since, a party of Papa-men came to dance the sword-dance at Lerwick as a public exhibition with great applause. The warlike dances of the northern people, of which I conceive this to be the only remnant in the British dominions,[1] are repeatedly alluded to by their poets and historians. The introduction of the Seven Champions savours of a later period, and was probably ingrafted upon the dance when *mysteries* and *moralities* (the first scenic representations) came into fashion. In a stall pamphlet, called the history of Buckshaven, it is said those fishers sprung from Danes, and brought with them their *war-dance* or *sword-dance*, and a rude wooden cut of it is given. We resist the hospitality of our entertainers, and return to Lerwick despite a most downright fall of rain. My pony stumbles coming down hill; saddle sways round, having, but one girth and that too long, and lays me on my back. *N.B.* The bogs in Zetland as soft as those in Liddisdale. Get to Lerwick about ten at night. No yacht has appeared.

[1]   Mr. W. S. Rose informs me that when he was at school at Winchester, the morris-dancers there used to exhibit a sword-dance resembling that described at Camacho's wedding in Don Quixote; and Mr. Morritt adds, that similar dances are even yet performed in villages about Rokeby every Christmas

8th August. — No yacht, and a rainy morning; bring up my journal. Day clears up, and we go to pay our farewell visits of thanks to the hospitable Lerwegians, at the Fort. Visit kind old Mr. Mowat, and walk him and Collector Ross to the point of Quaggers, or Twaggers, which forms one arm of the southern entrance, to the sound of Bressay. From the eminence a delightful sea view, with several of those narrow capes and deep reaches or inlets of the sea, which indent the shores of that land. On the right hand a narrow bay, bounded by the isthmus of Sound, with a house upon it resembling an old castle. In the indenture of the bay, and divided from the sea by a slight causeway, the lake of *Cleik-him-in*, with its Pictish castle. Beyond this the bay opens another yet; and, behind all, a succession of capes, headlands, and islands, as far as the cape called Sumburgh-head, which is the furthest point of Zetland in that direction. Inland, craggy, and sable muirs, with cairns, among which we distinguish the Wart or Ward of Wick, to which we walked on the 4th. On the left the island of Bressay, with its peaked hill called the Wart of Bressay. Over Bressay see the top of Hang-cliff. Admire the Bay of Lerwick, with its shipping, widening out to the northwards, and then again contracted into a narrow sound, through which the infamous Bothwell was pursued by Kirkaldy of Grange, until he escaped through the dexterity of his pilot, who sailed close along a sunken rock, upon which Kirkaldy, keeping the weather-gauge, struck, and sustained damage. The rock is visible at low water, and is still called the Unicorn, from the name of Kirkaldy's vessel. Admire Mr. Mowat's little farm, of about thirty acres, bought about twenty years since for £75, and redeemed from the miserable state of the surrounding country, so that it now bears excellent corn; here also was a hay crop. With Mr. Turnbull's it makes two. Visit Mr. Ross, collector of the customs, who presents me with the most superb collection of the stone axes (or adzes, or whatever they are), called *celts*. The Zetlanders call them *thunderbolts*, and keep them in their houses as a receipt against thunder; but the Collector has succeeded in obtaining several. We are now to dress for dinner with the Notables of Lerwick, who give us an entertainment in their Town Hall. Oho!

Just as we were going to dinner, the yacht appeared, and Mr. Stevenson landed. He gives a most favourable account of the isles to the northward, particularly Unst. I believe Lerwick is the worst part of Shetland. Are hospitably received and entertained by the Lerwick gentlemen. They are a quick intelligent race — chiefly Scottish birth, as appears from their names Mowat, Gifford, Scott, and so forth. These are the chief proprietors. The Norwegian or Danish surnames, though of course the more ancient, belong, with some exceptions, to the lower ranks. The Veteran Corps expects to be disbanded, and the officers and Lerwegians seem to part with regret. Some of the officers talk of settling here. The price of everything moderate, and the style of living unexpensive. Against these conveniences are to be placed a total separation from public life, news, and literature; and a variable and inhospitable climate. Lerwick will suffer most severely if the Fort is not occupied by some force or other; for, between whisky and frolic, the Greenland sailors will certainly burn the little town. We have seen a good deal, and heard much more, of the pranks of these unruly guests. A gentleman of Lerwick, who had company to dine with him, observed beneath his window a party of sailors eating a leg of roast mutton, which he witnessed with philanthropic satisfaction, till he received the melanchly information, that that individual leg of mutton, being the very sheet-anchor of his own entertainment, had been violently carried off from his kitchen, spit and all, by these honest gentlemen, who were now devouring it. Two others having carried off a sheep, were apprehended, and brought before a Justice of the Peace, who questioned them respecting the fact. The first denied he had take the sheep, but said he had seen it taken away by a fellow, with a red nose and a black wig — (this was the Justice's description) —" Don't you think he was like his honour Tom?" he added, appealing to his comrade. "By G—, Jack," answered Tom, "I believe it was the very man!" Erskine has been busy with these facetious gentlemen, and has sent several to prison, but nothing could have been done without the soldiery. We leave Lerwick at eight o'clock, and sleep on board the yacht.

9th August, 1814. — Waked at seven, and find the vessel has left Lerwick harbour, and is on the point of entering the sound which divides the small island of Mousa (or Queen's island) from Coningsburgh, a very wild part of the main island so called. Went ashore, and see the very ancient castle of Mousa, which stands close on the sea-shore. It is a Pictish fortress, the most entire probably in the world. In form it resembles a dice-box, for the truncated cone is continued only to a certain height, after which it begins to rise perpendicularly, or rather with a tendency to expand outwards. The building is round, and has been surrounded with an outer-wall, of which hardly the slightest vestiges now remain. It is composed of a layer of stones, without cement; they are not of large size, but rather small and thin. To give a vulgar comparison, it resembles an old ruinous pigeonhouse. Mr. Stevenson took the dimensions of this curious fort, which are as follows:— Outside diameter at the base is fifty-two feet; at the top thirty-eight feet. The diameter of the interior at the base is nineteen feet six inches; at the top twenty-one feet; the curve in the inside being the reverse of the outside, or nearly so. The thickness of the walls at the base seventeen feet; at the top eight feet six inches. The height outside forty-two feet; the inside thirty-four feet. The door or entrance faces the sea, and the interior is partly filled with rubbish. When you enter you see, in the inner wall, a succession of small openings like windows, directly one above another, with broad flat stones, serving for lintels; these are about nine inches thick. The whole resembles a ladder. There were four of these perpendicular rows of windows or apertures, the situation of which corresponds with the cardinal points of the compass. You enter the galleries contained in the thickness of the wall by two of these apertures, which have been broken down. These interior spaces are of two descriptions: one consists of a winding ascent, not quite an inclined plane, yet not by any means a regular stair; but the edges of the stones, being suffered to project irregularly, serve for rude steps — or a kind of assistance. Through this narrow staircase, which winds round the building, you creep up to the top of the castle, which is partly ruinous. But besides the staircase, there branch off at irregular intervals horizontal galleries, which go round the whole building, and receive air from the holes I formerly mentioned. These apertures vary in size, diminishing as they run, from about thirty inches in width by eighteen in height, till they are only about a foot square. The lower galleries are full man height, but narrow. They diminish both in height and width as they ascend, and as the thickness of the wall in which they are enclosed diminishes. The uppermost gallery is so narrow and low, that it was with great difficulty I crept through it. The walls are built very irregularly, the sweep of the cone being different on the different sides.

It is said by Torfæus that this fort was repaired and strengthened by Erlind, who, having forcibly carried off the mother of Harold Earl of the Orkneys resolved to defend himself to extremity in this place against the insulted Earl. How a castle could be defended which had no opening to the outside for shooting arrows, and which was of a capacity to be pulled to pieces by the assailants, who could advance without annoyance to the bottom of the wall (unless it were battlemented upon the top), does not easily appear. But to Erlind's operations the castle of Mousa possibly owes the upper and perpendicular, or rather overhanging, part of its elevation, and also its rude staircase. In these two particulars it seems to differ from all other Picts' castles, which are ascended by an inclined plane, and generally, I believe, terminate in a truncated cone, without that strange counterpart of the perpendicular or projecting part of the upper wall. Opposite to the castle of Mousa are the ruins of another Pictish fort: indeed, they all communicate with each other through the isles. The island of Mousa is the property of a Mr. Piper, who has improved it considerably, and values his castle. I advised him to clear out the interior, as he tells us there are three or four galleries beneath those now accessible, and the difference of height between the exterior and interior warrants his assertion.

We get on board, and in time, for the wind freshens, and becomes contrary. We beat down to Sumburgh-head, through rough weather. This is the extreme south-eastern point of Zetland; and as the Atlantic and German oceans unite at this point, a frightful tide runs here, called Sumburgh-rost. The breeze, contending with the tide, flings the breakers in great style upon the high broken cliffs of Sumburgh-head. They are all one white foam, ascending to a great height. We wished to double this point, and lie by in a bay between that and the northern or north-western cape, called Fitful-head, and which seems higher than Sumburgh itself — and tacked repeatedly with this view; but a confounded islet, called *The Horse*, always baffled us, and, after three heats, fairly distanced us. So we run into a roadstead, called Quendal bay, on the south-eastern side, and there anchor for the night. We go ashore with various purposes — Stevenson to see the site of a proposed lighthouse on this tremendous cape — Marjoribanks to shoot rabbits — and Duff and I to look about us.

I ascended the head by myself, which is lofty, and commands a wild sea-view. Zetland stretches away, with all its projecting capes and inlets, to the north-eastward. Many of those inlets approach each other very nearly; indeed, the two opposite bays at Sumburgh-head seem on the point of joining, and rendering that cape an island. The two creeks from those east and western seas are only divided by a low isthmus of blowing sand, and similar to that which wastes part of the east coast of Scotland. It has here blown like the deserts of Arabia, and destroyed some houses, formerly the occasional residences of the Earls of Orkney. The steep and rocky side of the cape, which faces the west, does seem much more durable. These lofty cliffs are all of sand-flag, a very loose and perishable kind of rock, which slides down in immense masses, like avalanches, after every storm. The rest lies so loose, that, on the very brow of the loftiest crag, I had no difficulty in sending down a fragment as large as myself: he thundered down in tremendous style, but splitting upon a projecting cliff, descended into the ocean like a shower of shrapnel shot. The sea beneath rages incessantly among a thousand of the fragments which have fallen from the peaks, and which assume an hundred strange shapes. It would have been a fine situation to compose an ode to the Genius of Sumburgh-head, or an Elegy upon a Cormorant — or to have written and spoken madness of any kind in prose or poetry. But I gave vent to my excited feelings in a more simple way; and sitting gently down on the steep green slope which led to the beach, I e'en slid down a few hundred feet, and found the exercise quite an adequate vent to my enthusiasm, I recommend this exercise (time and place suiting) to all my brother scribblers, and I have no doubt it will save much effusion of Christian ink. Those slopes are covered with beautiful short herbage. At the foot of the ascent, and towards the isthmus, is the old house of Sumburgh, in appearance a most dreary mansion. I found, on my arrival at the beach, that the hospitality of the inhabitants had entrapped my companions. I walked back to meet them, but escaped the gin and water. On board about nine o'clock at night. A little schooner lies between us and the shore, which we had seen all day buffeting the tide and breeze like ourselves. The wind increases, an the ship is made SNUG — a sure sign the passengers will not be so.

10th August, 1814. — The omen was but too true — a terrible combustion on board, among plates, dishes, glasses, writing-desks, etc. etc.; not a wink of sleep. We weigh and stand out into that delightful current called *Sumburgh-rost* or *rust*. This tide certainly owes us a grudge, for it drove us to the eastward about thirty miles on the night of the first, and occasioned our missing the Fair Isle, and now it has caught us on our return. All the landsmen sicker than sick, and our Viceroy, Stevenson, qualmish, This is the only time that I have felt more than temporary inconvenience, but this morning I have headache and nausea; these are trifles, and in a well-found vessel, with a good pilot, we have none of that mixture of danger which gives dignity to the traveller. But he must have a stouter heart than mine who can contemplate without horror the situation of a vessel of an inferior description caught among these headlands and reefs of rocks, in the long and dark winter nights of these regions. Accordingly, wrecks are frequent. It is proposed to have a light on Sumburgh-head, which is the first land made by vessels coming from the eastward; Fitful-head is higher, but is to the west, from which quarter few vessels come.

We are now clear of Zetland, and about ten o'clock reach the Fair Isle;[1] one of their boats comes off, a strange-looking thing without an entire plank in it, excepting one on each side, upon the strength of which the whole depends, the rest being patched and joined. This trumpery skiff the men manage with the most astonishing dexterity, and row with remarkable speed; they have two banks, that is, two rowers on each bench, and use very short paddles. The wildness of their appearance, with long elf-locks, striped worsted caps, and shoes of raw hide — the fragility of their boat — and their extreme curiosity about us and our cutter, give them a title to be distinguished as *natives*. One of our people told their steersman, by way of jeer, that he must have great confidence in Providence to go to sea in such a vehicle; the man very sensibly replied, that without the same confidence he would not go to sea in the best *tool* in England. We take to our boat, and row for about three miles round the coast, in order to land at the inhabited part of the island. This coast abounds with grand views of rocks and bays. One immense portion of rock is (like the Holm of

---

[1] This is a solitary island, lying about half-way between Orkney and Zetland.

Noss) separated by a chasm from the mainland. As it is covered with herbage on the top, though a literal precipice all round, the natives contrive to ascend the rock by a place which would make a goat dizzy, and then drag the sheep up by ropes, though they sometimes carry a sheep up on their shoulders. The captain of a sloop of war, being ashore while they were at this work, turned giddy and sick while looking at them. This immense precipice is several hundred feet high, and is perforated below by some extraordinary apertures, through which a boat might pass; the light shines distinctly through these hideous chasms.

After passing a square bay called the Northaven, tenanted by sea-fowl and seals (the first we have yet seen), we come in view of the small harbour. Land, and breakfast, for which, till now, none of us felt inclination. In front of the little harbour is the house of the tacksman, Mr. Strong, and in view are three small assemblages of miserable huts, where the inhabitants of the isle live. There are about thirty families and 250 inhabitants upon the *Fair Isle*. It merits its name, as the plain upon which the hamlets are situated, bears excellent barley, oats, and potatoes, and the rest of the isle is beautiful pasture, excepting to the eastward, where there is a moss, equally essential to the comfort of the inhabitants, since it supplies them with peats for fuel. The Fair Isle is about three miles long and a mile and a half broad. Mr. Strong received us very courteously. He lives here, like Robinson Crusoe, in absolute solitude as to society, unless by a chance visit from the officers of a man-of-war. There is a signal-post maintained on the island by Government, under this gentleman's inspection; when any ship appears that cannot answer his signals, he sends off to Lerwick and Kirkwall to give the alarm. Rogers[1] was off here last year, and nearly cut off one of Mr. Strong's expressboats, but the active islanders outstripped his people by speed of rowing. The inhabitants pay Mr. Strong for the possessions which they occupy under him as sub-tenants, and cultivate the isle in their own way, *i.e.* by digging instead of ploughing (though the ground is quite open and free from rocks, and they have several scores of ponies), and by raising alternate crops of barley, oats, and potatoes; the first and last are admirably good. They rather over-manure their crops; the possessions

[1]   An American Commodore.

lie runrig, that is, by alternate ridges, and the outfield or pasture ground is possessed as common to all their cows and ponies. The islanders fish for Mr. Strong at certain fixed rates, and the fish is his property, which he sends to Kirkwall, Lerwick, or elsewhere, in a little schooner, the same which we left in Quendal bay, and about the arrival of which we found them anxious. An equal space of rich land on the Fair Isle, situated in an inland county of Scotland, would rent for £3000 a year at the very least. To be sure it would not be burdened with the population of 250 souls, whose bodies (fertile as it is) it cannot maintain in bread, they being supplied chiefly from the mainland. Fish they have plenty, and are even nice in their choice. Skate they will not touch; dog-fish they say is only food for Orkney-men, and when they catch them, they make a point of tormenting the poor fish for eating off their baits from the hook, stealing the haddocks from their lines, and other enormities. These people, being about half-way between Shetland and Orkney, have unfrequent connexion with either archipelago, and live and marry entirely among themselves. One lad told me, only five persons had left the island since his remembrance, and of those, three were pressed for the navy. They seldom go to Greenland; but this year five or six of their young men were on board the whalers. They seemed extremely solicitous about their return, and repeatedly questioned us about the names of the whalers which were at Lerwick, a point on which we could give little information.

The manners of these islanders seem primitive and simple, and they are sober, good-humoured, and friendly — but *jimp* honest. Their comforts are, of course, much dependent on *their master's* pleasure; for so they call Mr. Strong. But they gave him the highest character for kindness and liberality, and prayed to God he might long be their ruler. After mounting the signal-post hill, or Malcolm's Head, which is faced by a most tremendous cliff, we separated on our different routes. The Sheriff went to rectify the only enormity on the island, which existed in the person of a drunken schoolmaster ; Marchie[1] went to shoot sea-fowl, or rather to frighten them, as his calumniators allege. Stevenson and Duff went to inspect the remains or vestiges of a Danish lighthouse upon a distant hill, called, as usual, the Ward, or Ward-hill, and returned with specimens of copper ore. Hamilton went

[1]   Mr. Marjoibanks.

down to cater fish for our dinner, and see it properly cooked — and I to see two remarkable indentures in the coast called *Rivas*, perhaps from their being rifted or *riven*. They are exactly like the Buller of Buchan, the sea rolling into a large open basin within the land through a natural archway. These places are close to each other — one is oblong, and it is easy to descend into it by a rude path; the other gulf is inaccessible from the land, unless to a *crags-man*, as these venturous climbers call themselves. I sat for about an hour upon the verge, like the cormorants around me, hanging my legs over the precipice; but I could not get free of two or three wellmeaning islanders, who held me fast by the skirts all the time — for it must be conceived, that our numbers and appointments had drawn out the whole population to admire and attend us. After we separated, each, like the nucleus of a comet, had his own distinct train of attendants. — Visit the capital town, a wretched assemblage of the basest huts, dirty without, and still dirtier within; pigs, fowls, cows, men, women, and children, all living promiscuously under the same roof, and in the same room — the brood-sow making (among the more opulent) a distinguished inhabitant of the mansion. The compost, a liquid mass of utter abomination, is kept in a square pond of seven feet deep; when I censured it, they allowed it might be dangerous to the *bairns*; but appeared unconscious of any other objection. I cannot wonder they want meal, for assuredly they waste it. A great *bowie* or wooden vessel of porridge is made in the morning; a child comes and sups a few spoonfuls; then Mrs. Sow takes her share; then the rest of the children or the parents, and all at pleasure; then come the poultry when the mess is more cool; the rest is flung upon the dunghill — and the goodwife wonders and complains when she wants meal in winter. They are a long-lived race, not withstanding utter and inconceivable dirt and sluttery. A man of sixty told me his father died only last year, aged ninety-eight; nor was this considered as very unusual.

The clergyman of Dunrossness, in Zetland, visits these poor people once a year, for a week or two during summer. In winter this is impossible, and even the summer visit is occasionally interrupted for two years. Marriages and baptisms are performed, as one of the Isles-men told me, *by the slump*, and one of the children was old enough to tell the clergyman who sprinkled him with water, "Deil be in your fingers." Last time, four couple were married; sixteen children baptized. The schoolmaster reads a portion of Scripture in the church each Sunday, when the clergyman is absent; but the present man is unfit for this part of his duty. The women knit worsted stockings, night-caps, and similar trifles, which they exchange with any merchant vessels that approach their lonely isle. In these respects they greatly regret the American war; and mention with unction the happy days when they could get from an American trader a bottle of peach-brandy or rum in exchange for a pair of worsted-stockings or a dozen of eggs. The humanity of their *master* interferes much with the favourite but dangerous occupation of the islanders, which is *fowling*, that is, taking the young sea-fowl from their nests among these tremendous crags. About a fortnight before we arrived, a fine boy of fourteen had dropped from the cliff, while in prosecution of this amusement, into a roaring surf, by which he was instantly swallowed up. The unfortunate mother was labouring at the peat-moss at a little distance. These accidents do not, however, strike terror into the survivors. They regard the death of an individual engaged in these desperate exploits, as we do the fate of a brave relation who falls in battle, when the honour of his death furnishes a balm to our sorrow. It therefore requires all the tacksman's authority to prevent a practice so pregnant with danger. Like all other precarious and dangerous employments, the occupation of the crags-men renders them unwilling to labour at employments of a more steady description. The Fair Isle inhabitants are a good-looking race, more like Zetlanders than Orkneymen. Evenson, and other names of a Norwegian or Danish derivation, attest their Scandinavian descent. Return and dine at Mr. Strong's, having sent our cookery ashore, not to overburthen his hospitality. In this place, and perhaps in the very cottage now inhabited by Mr. Strong, the Duke of Medina Sidonia, Commander-in-Chief of the Invincible Armada, wintered, after losing his vessel to the eastward of the island. It was not till he had spent some weeks in this miserable abode, that he got off to Norway. Independently of the moral consideration, that, from the pitch of power in which he stood a few days before, the proudest peer of the proudest nation in Europe found himself dependent on the jealous and scanty charity of these secluded islanders, it is scarce possible not to reflect with compassion on the change of situation from the palaces of Estramadura to the hamlet of the Fair Isle

> Dost thou wish for thy deserts, 0 Son of Hodeirah?
>
> Dost thou long for the gales of Arabia? [1]

Mr. Strong gave me a curious old chair belonging to Quendale, a former proprietor of the Fair Isle, and which a more zealous antiquary would have dubbed " the Duke's chair." I will have it refitted for Abbotsford, however. About eight o'clock we take boat, amid the cheers of the inhabitants, whose minds, subdued by our splendour, had been secured by our munificence, which consisted in a moderate benefaction of whisky and tobacco, and a few shillings laid out on their staple commodities. They agreed no such day had been seen in the isle. The signal-post displayed its flags, and to recompense these distinguished marks of honour, we hung out our colours, stood into the bay, and saluted with three guns,

> Echoing from a thousand caves,

and then bear away for Orkney, leaving, if our vanity does not deceive us, a very favourable impression on the mind of the inhabitants of the Fair Isle. The tradition of the Fair Isle is unfavourable to those shipwrecked strangers, who are said to have committed several acts of violence to extort the supplies of provision, given them sparingly and with reluctance by the islanders, who were probably themselves very far from well supplied.

I omitted to say we were attended in the morning by two very sportive whales, but of a kind, as some of our crew who had been on board Greenland-men assured us, which it was very dangerous to attack. There were two Gravesend smacks fishing off the isle. Lord, what a long draught London makes !

11th August, 1814. — After a sound sleep to make amends for last night, we find, at awaking, the vessel off the Start of Sanda, the first land in the Orkneys which we could make. There a lighthouse has been erected lately upon the best construction. Landed and surveyed it. All in excellent order, and the establishment of the keepers in the same style of comfort and respectability as elsewhere, far better than the house of the master of the Fair Isle, and rivalling my own baronial mansion of Abbotsford. Go to the top of the tower and survey the island, which, as the name implies, is level, flat, and sandy, quite the

---

[1]   Thalaba, Book viii.

Lighthouse, Isle of Sandy

reverse of those in Zetland: it is intersected by creeks and small lakes, and, though it abounds with shell marle, seems barren. There is one dreadful inconvenience of an island life, of which we had here an instance. The keeper's wife had an infant in her arms — her first-born, too, of which the poor woman had been delivered without assistance. Erskine told us of a horrid instance of malice which had been practised in this island of Sanda. A decent tenant, during the course of three or four successive years, lost to the number of twenty-five cattle, stabbed as they lay in their fold by some abominable wretch. What made the matter stranger was, that the poor man could not recollect any reason why he should have had the ill-will of a single being, only that in taking up names for the *militia*, a duty imposed upon him by the Justices, he thought he might possibly have given some unknown offence. The villain was never discovered.

The wrecks on this coast were numerous before the erection of the lighthouse. It was not uncommon to see five or six vessels on shore at once. The goods and chattels of the inhabitants are all said to savour of *Flotsome* and *Jetsome*, as the floating wreck and that which is driven ashore are severally called. Mr. Stevenson happened to observe that the boat of a Sanda farmer had bad sails — "If it had been His (*i.e.* God's) will that you hadna built sae many lighthouses hereabout "— answered the Orcadian, with great composure —," I would have had new sails last winter." Thus do they talk and think upon these subjects; and so talking and thinking, I fear the poor mariner has little chance of any very anxious attempt to assist him. There is one wreck, a Danish vessel, now aground under our lee. These Danes are the stupidest seamen, by all accounts, that sail the sea. When this light upon the Start of Sanda was established, the Commissioners, with laudable anxiety to extend its utility, had its description and bearings translated into Danish and sent to Copenhagen. But they never attend to such trifles. The Norwegians are much better liked, as a clever, hardy, sensible people. I forgot to notice there was a Norwegian prize lying in the Sound of Lerwick, sent in by one of our cruisers. This was a queer-looking, half-decked vessel, all tattered and torn, and shaken to pieces, looking like Coleridge's Spectre Ship. It was pitiable to see such a prize. Our servants went aboard, and got one of their loaves, and gave a dreadful account of its composition. I got and cut a crust of it; it was rye-bread, with a slight mixture of pine-fir bark or sawings of deal. It was not good, but (as Charles XII said) might be eaten. But after all, if the people can be satisfied with such bread as this, it seems hard to interdict it to them. What would a Londoner say if, instead of his roll and muffins, this black bread, relishing of tar and turpentine, were presented for his breakfast? I would to God there could be a Jehovah-jireh, " a ram caught in the thicket," to prevent the sacrifice of that people.

The few friends who may see this journal are much indebted for these pathetic remarks to the situation under which they are recorded; for since we left the lighthouse we have been struggling with adverse wind (pretty high too), and a very strong tide, called the Rost of the Start, which, like Sumburgh Rost, bodes no good to our roast and boiled. The worst is that this struggle carries us past a most curious spectacle, being no less than the carcases of two hundred and sixty-five whales, which have been driven ashore in Taftsness bay, now lying close under us. With all the inclination in the world, it is impossible to stand in close enough to verify this massacre of Leviathans with our own eyes, as we do not care to run the risk of being drawn ashore ourselves among the party. In fact, this species of spectacle has been of late years very common among the isles. Mr. Stevenson saw upwards of a hundred and fifty whales lying upon the shore in a bay at Unst, in his northward trip. They are not large, but are decided whales, measuring perhaps from fifteen to twenty-five feet. They are easily mastered, for the first that is wounded among the sounds and straits so common in the isles, usually runs ashore. The rest follow the blood, and, urged on by the boats behind, run ashore also. A cut with one of the long whaling knives under the back-fin is usually fatal to these huge animals. The two hundred and sixty-five whales, now lying within two or three miles of us, were driven ashore by seven boats only.

Five o'clock. — We are out of the *Rost* (I detest that word), and driving fast through a long, sound among low green islands, which hardly lift themselves above the sea — not a cliff or hill to be seen — what a contrast to the land we have left! We are standing for some creek or harbour, called Lingholm bay, to lie to or anchor for the night; for to pursue our course by night, and that a thick one, among these isles, and islets, and sandbanks, is out of the question—clear moonlight might do. Our sea is now moderate. But, oh gods and men! what misfortunes have travellers to record! Just as the quiet of the elements had reconciled us to the thought of dinner, we learn that an unlucky sea has found its way into the galley during the last infernal combustion, when the lee-side and bolt-sprit were constantly under water; so our soup is poisoned with salt water — our cod and haddocks, which cost ninepence this blessed morning, and would have been worth a couple of guineas in London, are soused in their primitive element — the curry is undone — and all gone to the devil. We all apply ourselves to comfort our Lord High Admiral Hamilton, whose despair for himself and the public might edify a patriot. His good-humour — which has hitherto defied every incident, aggravated even by the gout — supported by a few bad puns, and a great many fair promises on the part of the steward and cook, fortunately restores his equilibrium.

Eight o'clock. — Our supplemental dinner proved excellent, and we have glided into an admirable roadstead or harbour, called Lingholm bay, formed by the small island of Lingholm embracing a small basin dividing that islet from the larger isle of Stronsay. Both, as well as Sanda, Eda, and others which we have passed, are low, green, and sandy. I have seen nothing to-day worth marking, except the sporting, of a very large whale at some distance, and H.'s face — at the news of the disaster in the cook-room. We are to weigh at two in the morning, and hope to reach Kirkwall, the capital of Orkney, by breakfast to-morrow. I trust there are no *rusts* or *rosts* in the road. I shall detest that word even when used to signify verd-antique or patina in the one sense, or roast venison in the other. Orkney shall begin a new volume of these exquisite memoranda.

OMISSION.— At Lerwick the Dutch fishers had again appeared on their old haunts. A very interesting meeting took place between them and the Lerwegians, most of them being old acquaintances. They seemed very poor, and talked of having been pillaged of everything by the French, and expected to have found Lerwick ruined by the war. They have all the careful, quiet, and economical habits of their country, and go on board their busses with the utmost haste so soon as they see the Greenland sailors, who usually insult and pick quarrels with them. The great amusement of the Dutch sailors is to hire the little ponies, and ride up and down upon them. On one occasion, a good many years ago, an English sailor interrupted this cavalcade, frightened the horses, and one or two Dutchmen got tumbles. Incensed at this beyond their usual moderation, they pursued the cause of their overthrow, and wounded him with one of their knives. The wounded man went on board his vessel, the crew of which, about fifty strong, came ashore with their long flinching knives with which they cut up the whales, and falling upon the Dutchmen, though twice their numbers, drove them all into the sea, where such as could not swim were in some risk of being drowned. The instance of aggression, or rather violent retaliation, on their part, is almost solitary. In general they are extremely quiet, and employ themselves in bartering their little merchandise of gin and gingerbread for Zetland hose and night-caps.

12th August, 1814. — With a good breeze and calm sea we weighed at two in the morning, and worked by short tacks up to Kirkwall bay, and find ourselves in that fine basin upon rising in the morning. The town looks well from the sea, but is chiefly indebted to the huge old cathedral that rises out of the centre. Upon landing we find it but a poor and dirty place, especially towards the harbour. Farther up the town are seen some decent old-fashioned houses, and the Sheriff's interest secures us good lodgings. Marchie goes to hunt for a pointer. The morning, which was rainy, clears up pleasantly, and Hamilton, Erskine, Duff, and I walk to Malcolm Laing's, who has a pleasant house about half a mile from the town. Our old acquaintance, though an invalid, received us kindly; he looks very poorly, and cannot walk without assistance, but seems to retain all the quick, earnest, and vivacious intelligence of his character and manner. After this visit the antiquities of the place, viz. the Bishop's palace, the Earl of Orkney's castle, and the cathedral, all situated within a stone-cast of each other. The two former are ruinous. The most prominent part of the ruins of the Bishop's palace is a large round tower, similar to that of Bothwell in architecture, but not equal to it in size. This was built by Bishop Reid, *tempore Jacobi V.*, and there is a rude statue of him in a niche in the front. At the north-east corner of the building is a square tower of greater antiquity, called the Mense or Mass Tower; but, as well as a second and smaller round tower, it is quite ruinous. A suite of apartments of different sizes fills up the space between these towers, all now ruinous. The building is said to have been of great antiquity, but was certainly in a great measure re-edified in the sixteenth century.

Fronting this castle or palace of the Bishop, and about a gun-shot distant, is that of the Earl of Orkney. The Earl's palace was built by Patrick Stewart, Earl of Orkney, the same who erected that of Scalloway, in Shetland. It is an elegant structure, partaking at once of the character of a palace and castle. The building forms three sides of an oblong square, but one of the sides extends considerably beyond the others. The great hall must have been remarkably handsome, opening into two or three huge rounds or turrets, the lower part of which is divided by stone shafts into three windows. It has two immense chimneys, the arches or lintels of which are formed by a flat arch, as at Crichton Castle. There is another very handsome apartment communicating with the hall like a modern drawing-room, and which has, like the former, its projecting turrets. The hall is lighted by a fine Gothic-shafted window at one end, and by others on the sides. It is approached by a spacious and elegant staircase of three flights of steps. The dimensions may be sixty feet long, twenty broad, and fourteen high, but doubtless an arched roof sprung from the side walls, so that fourteen feet was only the height from the round to the arches. Any modern architect, wishing to emulate the real Gothic architecture, and apply it to the purposes of modern splendour, might derive excellent hints from this room. The exterior ornaments are also extremely elegant. The ruins, once the residence of this haughty and oppressive Earl, are now so disgustingly nasty, that it required all the zeal of an antiquary to prosecute the above investigation. Architecture seems to have been Earl Patrick's prevailing taste. Besides this castle and that of Scalloway, he added to or enlarged the old castle of Bressay. To accomplish these objects, he oppressed the people with severities unheard-of even in that oppressive age, drew down on himself a shameful though deserved punishment, and left these dishonoured ruins to hand down to posterity the tale of his crimes and of his fall. We may adopt, though in another sense, his own presumptuous motto — *Sic Fuit, Est, et Erit.*

We visit the cathedral, dedicated to St. Magnus, which greeted the Sheriff's approach with a merry peal. Like that of Glasgow, this church has escaped the blind fury of Reformation. It was founded in

St Magnus Cathedral, Orkney

1138, by Ronald, Earl of Orkney, nephew of the Saint. It is of great size, being 260 feet long, or thereabout, and supported by twenty-eight Saxon pillars, of good workmanship. The round arch predominates in the building, but I think not exclusively. The steeple (once a very high spire) rises upon four pillars of great strength, which occupy each angle of the nave. Being destroyed by lightning, it was rebuilt upon a low and curtailed plan. The appearance of the building is rather massive and gloomy than elegant, and many of the exterior ornaments, carving around the doorways, etc., have been injured by time. We entered the cathedral, the whole of which is kept locked, swept and in good order, although only the eastern end is used for divine worship. We walked some time in the nave and western end, which is left unoccupied, and has a very solemn effect as the avenue to the place of worship. There were many tombstones on the floor and elsewhere some, doubtless, of high antiquity. One, I remarked, had the shield of arms hung by the corner, with a helmet above it of a large proportion, such as I have seen on the most ancient seals. But we had neither time nor skill to decipher what noble Orcadian lay beneath. The church is as well fitted up as could be expected; much of the old carved oak remains, but with a motley mixture of modern deal pews. All, however, is neat and clean, and does great honour to the kirk-session who maintain its decency. I remarked particularly Earl Patrick's seat, adjoining to that of the magistrates, but surmounting it and every other in the church; it is surrounded with a carved screen of oak, rather elegant, and bears his arms and initials, and the motto I have noticed. He bears the royal arms *without any mark of bastardy* (his father was a natural son of James V.) quarterly, with a lymphad or galley, the ancient arms of the county. This circumstance was charged against him on his trial.[1] I understand the late Mr. Gilbert

[1] This noted oppressor was finally brought to trial, and beheaded at the Cross of Edinburgh [6th February 1614]. It is said that the King's mood was considerably heated against him by some ill-chosen and worse written Latin inscriptions with which his father and himself had been unlucky enough to decorate some of their insular palaces. In one of these, Earl Robert, the father, had given his own designation thus:- "Orcadiæ Comes Rex Jacobi Quinti Filius." In this case he was not, perhaps, guilty of anything worse than bad Latin. But James VI., who had a keen nose for puzzling out treason, and with whom an assault and battery upon Priscian ranked in nearly the same degree of crime, had little doubt that the use of the nominative *Rex*, instead of the genitive *Regis*, had a treasonable savour.' - Scott's Miscellaneous Prose Works, vol. xxiii. p.232.

Laing Meason left the interest of £1000 to keep up this cathedral.

There are in the street facing the cathedral the ruins of a much more ancient castle; a proper feudal fortress belonging to the Earls of Orkney, but called the King's Castle. It appears to have been very strong, being situated near the harbour, and having, as appears from the fragments, very massive walls. While the wicked Earl Patrick was in confinement, one of his natural sons defended this castle to extremity against the King's troops, and only surrendered when it was nearly a heap of ruins, and then under condition he should not be brought in evidence against his father.

We dine at the inn, and drink the Prince Regent's health, being that of the day — Mr. Baikie of Tankerness dines with us.

13th August, 1814. — A bad morning, but clears up. No letters from Edinburgh. The country about Kirkwall is flat, and tolerably cultivated. We see oxen generally wrought in the small country carts, though they have a race of ponies, like those of Shetland, but larger. Marchie goes to shoot on a hill called Whiteford, which slopes away about two or three miles from Kirkwall. The grouse is abundant, for the gentleman who chaperons Marchie killed thirteen brace and a half, with a snipe. There are no partridges nor hares. The soil of Orkney is better, and its air more genial than Shetland but it is far less interesting and, possesses none of the wild and peculiar character of the more northern archipelago. All vegetables grow here freely in the gardens, and there are one or two attempts at trees where they are sheltered by walls. How ill they succeed may be conjectured from our bringing with us a qualtity of brushwood, commissioned by Malcolm Laing from Aberbrothock, to be sticks to his pease. This trash we brought two hundred miles. I have little to add, except that the Orkney people have some odd superstitions about a stone on which they take oaths to Odin. Lovers often perform this ceremony in pledge of mutual faith, and are said to account it a sacred engagement. — It is agreed that we go on board after dinner, and sail with the next tide. The magistrates of Kirkwall present us with the freedom of their ancient burgh; and Erskine, instead of being cumbered with drunken sailors, as at Lerwick, or a drunken schoolmaster, as at Fair Isle, is annoyed by his own Substitute. This will occasion his remaining two days at Kirkwall, during which time it is proposed we shall visit the lighthouse upon the dangerous rocks called the Skerries, in the Pentland Firth; and then, returning to the eastern side of Pomona, take up the counsellor at Stromness. It is further settled that we leave Marchie with Erskine to get another day's shooting. On board at ten o'clock, after a little bustle in expediting our domestics, washerwomen, etc.

14th August, 1814. — Sail about four, and in rounding the mainland of Orkney, called Pomona, encounter a very heavy sea; about ten o'clock, get into the Sound of Holm or Ham, a fine smooth current meandering away between two low green islands, which have little to characterise them. On the right of the Sound is the mainland, and a deep bay called Scalpa Flow indents it up to within two miles of Kirkwall. A canal through this neck of the island would be of great consequence to the burgh. We see the steeple and church of Kirkwall across the island very distinctly. Getting out of the Sound of Holm, we stand in to the harbour or roadstead of Widewall, where we find seven or eight foreign vessels bound for Ireland, and a sloop belonging to the lighthouse service. These roadsteads are common all through the Orkneys, and afford excellent shelter for small vessels. The day is pleasant and sunny, but the breeze is too high to permit landing at the Skerries. Agree, therefore, to stand over for the mainland of Scotland, and visit Thurso. Enter the Pentland Firth, so celebrated for the strength and fury of its tides, which is boiling even in this pleasant weather; we see a large ship battling with this heavy current, and though with all her canvas set and a breeze, getting more and more involved. See the two Capes of Dungsby or Duncansby, and Dunnet-head, between which lies the celebrated John o' Groat's house, on the north-eastern extremity of Scotland. The shores of Caithness rise bold and rocky before us, a contrast to the Orkneys, which are all low, excepting the Island of Hoy. On Duncansby-head appear some remarkable rocks, like towers, called the Stacks of Duncansby. Near this shore runs the remarkable breaking tide called the *Merry Men of Mey*, whence Mackenzie takes the scenery of a poem —

> Where the dancing Men of Mey,
> Speed the current to the land. [1]

[1]   Henry Mackenzie's Introduction to 'The Fatal Sisters.' - Works, 1808, Vol. viii. p. 63.

Here, according to his locality, the Caithness man witnessed the vision, in which was introduced the song translated by Gray, under the title of the Fatal Sisters. On this subject, Mr. Baikie told me the following remarkable circumstance: — A clergyman told him, that while some remnants of the Norse were yet spoken in North Ronaldsha, he carried thither the translation of Mr. Gray, then newly published, and read it to some of the old people as referring to the ancient history of their islands. But so soon as he had proceeded a little way, they exclaimed they knew it very well in the original, and had often sung it to himself when he asked them for an old Norse song; they called it *The Enchantresses*. — The breeze dies away between two wicked little islands called Swona and Stroma, the latter belonging to Caithness, the former to Orkney.

— *Nota Bene*. The inhabitants of the rest of the Orcades despise those of Swona for eating limpets, as being the last of human meannesses. Every land has its fashions. The Fair-Islesmen disdain Orkney-men for eating dog-fish. Both islands have dangerous reefs and whirlpools, where, even, in this fine day, the tide rages furiously. Indeed, the large high unbroken billows, which at every swell hide from our deck each distant object, plainly intimate what a dreadful current this must be when vexed by high or adverse winds. Finding ourselves losing ground in the tide, and unwilling to waste time, we give up Thurso — run back into the roadstead or bay of Long-Hope, and anchor under the fort. The bay has four entrances and safe anchorage in most winds, and having become a great rendezvous for shipping (there are nine vessels lying here at present), has been an object of attention with Government.

Went ashore after dinner, and visited the fort, which is only partly completed; it is a *flêche* to the sea, with eight guns, twenty-four pounders, but without any land defences; the guns are mounted *en barbette*, without embrasures, each upon a kind of moveable stage, which stage wheeling upon a pivot in front, and traversing by means of wheels behind, can be pointed in any direction that may be thought necessary. Upon this stage, the gun-carriage moves forward and recoils, and the depth of the parapet shelters the men even better than an embrasure; at a little distance from this battery they are building a Martello tower, which is to cross the fire of the battery, and also that of another projected tower upon the opposite point of the bay. The expedience of these towers seems excessively problematical. Supposing them impregnable, or nearly so, a garrison of fourteen or fifteen men may be always blockaded by a very trifling number, while the enemy dispose of all in the vicinity at their pleasure. In the case of Long-Hope, for instance, a frigate might disembark 100 men, take the fort in the rear, where it is undefended even by a palisade, destroy the magazines, spike and dismount the cannon, carry off or cut out any vessels in the roadstead, and accomplish all the purposes that could bring them to so remote a spot, in spite of a serjeant's party in the Martello tower, and without troubling themselves about them at all. Meanwhile, Long-Hope will one day turn out a flourishing place; there will soon be taverns and slop-shops, where sailors rendezvous in such numbers; then will come quays, docks, and warehouses; and then a thriving town. Amen, so be it. This is the first fine day we have enjoyed to an end since Sunday, 31st ult. Rainy, cold, and hazy have been our voyages around these wild islands; I hope the weather begins to mend, though Mr. Wilson, our master, threatens a breeze to-morrow. We are to attempt the Skerries, if possible; if not, we will, I believe, go to Stromness.

15th August, 1814. — Fine morning; we get again into the Pentland Firth, and with the aid of a pilot-boat belonging to the lighthouse service, from South Ronaldsha, we attempt the Skerries. Notwithstanding the fair weather, we have a specimen of the violence of the floodtide, which forms whirlpools on the shallow sunken rocks by the islands of Swona and Stroma, and in the deep water makes strange, smooth, whirling, and swelling eddies, called by the sailors *wells*. We run through the *wells of Tuftile* in particular, which, in the least stress of weather, wheel a large ship round and round, without respect either to helm or sails. Hence the distinction of *wells* and *waves* in old English; the well being that smooth, glassy, oily-looking eddy, the force of which seems to the eye almost resistless. The bursting of the waves in foam around these strange eddies has a bewildering and confused appearance, which it is impossible to describe. Get off the Skerries about ten o'clock, and land easily; it is the first time a boat has got there for several days. The Skerries[1] is an island about sixty

---

[1] 'A Skerrie means a flattish rock which the sea does not overflow.' — *Edmondstone's View of the Zetlands.*

acres, of fine short herbage, belonging to Lord Dundas; it is surrounded by a reef of precipitous rocks, not very high, but inaccessible, unless where the ocean has made ravines among them, and where stairs have been cut down to the water for the lighthouse service. Those inlets have a romantic appearance, and have been christened by the sailors, the Parliament House, the Seals' Lying-in-Hospital, etc. The last inlet, after rushing through a deep chasm, which is open overhead, is continued underground, and then again opens to the sky in the middle of the island: in this hole the seals bring out their whelps; when the tide is high, the waves rise up through this aperture in the middle of the isle — like the blowing of a whale in noise and appearance. There is another round cauldron of solid rock, to which the waves have access through a natural arch in the rock, having another and lesser arch rising above it; in hard weather, the waves rush through both apertures with a horrid noise; the workmen called it the Carron Blast, and indeed, the variety of noises which issued from the abyss, somewhat reminded me of that engine. Take my rifle, and walk round the cliffs in search of seals, but see none, and only disturb the digestion of certain aldermen-cormorants, who were sitting on the points of the crags after a good fish breakfast; only made one good shot out of four. The lighthouse is too low, and on the old construction, yet it is of the last importance. The keeper is an old man-of-war's-man, of whom Mr. Stevenson observed that he was a great swearer when he first came; but after a year or two's residence in this solitary abode, became a changed man. There are about fifty head of cattle on the island; they must be got in and off with great danger and difficulty. There is no water upon the isle, except what remains after rain in some pools; these sometimes dry in summer, and the cattle are reduced to great straits. Leave the isle about one; and the wind and tide being favourable, crowd all sail, and get on at the rate of fourteen miles an hour. Soon reach our old anchorage at the Long-Hope, and passing, stand to the north-westward, up the sound of Hoy, for Stromness.

I should have mentioned that in going down the Pentland Firth this morning we saw Johnnie Groat's house, or rather the place where it stood, now occupied by a storehouse. Our pilot opines there was no such man as Johnnie Groat, for, he says, he cannot hear that anybody *ever saw him*. This reasoning would put down most facts of antiquity. They gather shells on the shore, called *Johnnie Groat's buckies*, but I cannot procure any at present. I may, also add, that the interpretation given to *wells* may apply to the *Wells of Slain*, in the fine ballad of Clerk Colvill; such eddies in the romantic vicinity of Slains Castle would be a fine place for a mermaid.[1]

Our wind fails us, and what is worse, becomes westerly; the Sound has now the appearance of a fine landlocked bay, the passages between the several islands being scarce visible. We have a superb view of Kirkwall Cathedral, with a strong gleam of sunshine upon it. Gloomy weather begins to collect around us, particularly on the island of Hoy, which, covered with gloom and vapour, now assumes a majestic mountainous character. On Pomona we pass the Hill of Orphir, which reminds me of the clergyman of that parish, who was called to account for some of his inaccuracies to the General Assembly; one charge he held particularly cheap, viz. that of drunkenness. "Reverend Moderator," said he, in reply, " I *do* drink, as other gentlemen do." This Orphir of the north must not be confounded with the Ophir of the south. From the latter came gold, silver, and precious stones; the former seems to produce little except peats. Yet these are precious commodities, which some of the Orkney Isles altogether want, and lay waste and burn the turf of their land instead of importing coal from Newcastle. The Orcadians seem by no means an alert or active race; they neglect the excellent fisheries which lie under their very noses, and in their mode of managing their boats, as well as in the general tone of urbanity and intelligence, are excelled by the less favoured Zetlanders. I observe they always crowd their boat with people in the bows, being the ready way to send her down in any awkward circumstance. There are remains of their Norwegian descent and language in North Ronaldsha, an isle I regret we did not see. A missionary preacher came ashore there a year or two since, but

[1] Clerk Colvill falls a sacrifice to a meeting with 'a fair Mermaid,' whom he found washing her 'Sark of Silk ' on this romantic shore. He had been warned by his 'gay lady' in these words:-

> O promise me now, Clerk Colvill,
> Or it will cost ye muckle strife,
> Ride never by the Wells of Slane,
> If ye wad live and brook your life.

being a very little black-bearded unshaved man, the seniors of the isle suspected him of being an ancient Pecht or Pict, and *no canny*, of course. The schoolmaster came down to entreat our worthy Mr. Stevenson, then about to leave the island, to come up and verify whether the preacher was an ancient Pecht, yea or no. Finding apologies were in vain, he rode up to the house where the unfortunate preacher, after three nights' watching, had got to bed, little conceiving under what odious suspicion he had fallen. As Mr. S. declined disturbing him, his boots were produced, which being a *little - little - very little* pair, confirmed, in the opinion of all the bystanders, the suspicion of Pechtism. Mr. S. therefore found it necessary to go into the poor man's sleeping apartment, where he recognised one Campbell, heretofore an ironmonger in Edinburgh, but who had put his hand for some years to the missionary plough; of course he warranted his quondam acquaintance to be no ancient Pecht. Mr. Stevenson carried the same schoolmaster who figured in the adventure of the Pecht, to the mainland of Scotland, to be examined for his office. He was extremely desirous to see a tree; and, on seeing one, desired to know what girss it was that grew at the top on't - the leaves appearing to him to be grass. They still speak a little Norse, and indeed I hear every day words of that language; for instance, *Ja, kul*, for "Yes, sir." We creep slowly up Hoy Sound, working under the Pomona shore; but there is no hope of reaching Stromness till we have the assistance of the evening tide. The channel now seems like a Highland loch; not the least ripple on the waves. The passage is narrowed, and (to the eye) blocked up by the interposition of the green and apparently fertile isle of Græmsay, the property of Lord Armadale.[1] Hoy looks yet grander, from comparing its black and steep mountains with this verdant isle. To add to the beauty of the Sound, it is rendered lively by the successive appearance of seven or eight whaling vessels from Davies' Straits ; large strong ships, which pass successively, with all their sails set, enjoying the little wind that is. Many of these vessels display the *garland*; that is, a wreath of ribbons which the young fellows on board have got from their sweethearts, or come by otherwise, and which hangs between the foremast and mainmast,

---

[1]   Sir William Honeyman, Bart. - a Judge of the Court of Session by the title of Lord Armadale.

surmounted sometimes by a small model of the vessel. This garland is hung up upon the 1st May, and remains till they come into port. I believe we shall dodge here till the tide makes about nine, and then get into Stromness: no boatman or sailor in Orkney thinks of the wind in comparison of the tides and currents. We must not complain, though the night gets rainy, and the Hill of Hoy is now completely invested with vapour and mist. In the forepart of the day we executed very cleverly a task of considerable difficulty and even danger.

16th August, 1814. — Get into Stromness bay, and anchor before the party are up. A most decided rain all night. The bay is formed by a deep indention in the mainland, or Pomona; on one side of which stands Stromness — a fishing village and harbour of *call* for the Davies' Straits whalers, as Lerwick is for the Greenlanders. Betwixt the vessels we met yesterday, seven or eight which passed us this morning, and several others still lying in the bay, we have seen between twenty and thirty of these large ships in this remote place. The opposite side of Stromness bay is protected by Hoy, and Græmsay lies between them; so that the bay seems quite land-locked, and the contrast between the mountains of Hoy, the soft verdure of Græmsay, and the swelling hill of Orphir on the mainland, has a beautiful effect. The day clears up, and Mr. Rae, Lord Armadale's factor, comes off from his house, called Clestrom, upon the shore opposite to Stromness, to breakfast with us. We go ashore with him. His farm is well cultivated, and he has procured an excellent breed of horses from Lanarkshire, of which county he is a native; strong hardy Galloways, fit for labour or hacks. By this we profited, as Mr. Rae mounted us all, and we set off to visit the Standing Stones of Stenhouse or Stennis.

At the upper end of the bay, about half-way between Clestrom and Stromness, there extends a loch of considerable size, of fresh water, but communicating with the sea by apertures left in a long bridge or causeway which divides them. After riding about two miles along this lake, we open another called the Loch of Harray, of about the same dimensions, and communicating with the lower lake, as the former does with the sea, by a stream, over which is constructed a causeway, with openings to suffer the flow and reflux of the water, as both lakes are affected by the tide. Upon the tongues of land which, approaching each other, divide the lakes of Stennis and Harray, are situated the

Standing Stones. The isthmus on the on the eastern side exhibits a semicircle of immensely large upright pillars of unhewn stone, surrounded by a mound of earth. As the mound is discontinued, it does not seem that the circle was ever completed. The flat or open part of the semicircle looks up a plain, where, at a distance, is seen a large tumulus. The highest of these stones may be about sixteen or seventeen feet, and I think there are none so low as twelve feet. At irregular distances are pointed out other unhewn pillars of the same kind. One, a little to the westward, is perforated with a round hole, perhaps to bind a victim; or rather, I conjecture, for the purpose of solemnly attesting the deity, a ring, — vide Eyrbiggia Saga. Several barrows are scattered around this strange monument. Upon the opposite isthmus is a complete circle, of ninety-five paces in diameter, surrounded by standing stones, less in size than the others, being only from ten or twelve to fourteen feet in height, and four in breadth. A deep trench is drawn around this circle on the outside of the pillars, and four tumuli, or mounds of earth, are regularly placed, two on each side.

Stonehenge excels these monuments, but I fancy they are otherwise unparalleled in Britain. The idea that such circles were exclusively Druidical is now justly exploded. The northern nations all used such erections to mark their places of meeting, whether for religious purposes or civil policy ; and there is repeated mention of them in the Sagas. See the Eyrbiggia Saga,[1] for the establishment of the Helga-fels, or holy mount, where the people held their Comitia, and where sacrifices were offered to Thor and Woden. About the centre of the semicircle is a broad flat stone, probably once the altar on which human victims were sacrificed. — Mr. Rae seems to think the common people have no tradition of the purpose of these stones, but probably he has not enquired particularly. He admits they look upon them with superstitious reverence; and it is evident that those which have fallen down (about half the original number) have been wasted by time, and not demolished. The materials of these monuments lay near, for the shores and bottom of the lake are of the same kind of rock. How they were raised, transported, and placed upright, is a puzzling question. In our ride back, noticed a round entrenchment, or tumulus, called the Hollow of Tongue.

[1]   Miscellaneous Prose Works, vol. v. p. 355.

The hospitality of Mrs. Rae detained us to an early dinner at Clestrom. About four o'clock took our longboat and rowed down the bay to visit the Dwarfie Stone of Hoy. We have all day been pleased with the romantic appearance of that island, for although the Hill of Hoy is not very high, perhaps about 1200 feet, yet rising perhaps pendicularly (almost) from the sea, and being very steep and furrowed with ravines, and catching all the mists from the western ocean, it has a noble and picturesque effect in every point of view. We land upon the island, and proceed up a long and very swampy valley broken into peat-bogs. The one side of this valley is, formed by the Mountain of Hoy, the other by another steep hill, having at the top a circular belt of rock; upon the slope of this last hill, and just where the principal mountain opens into a wide and precipitous and circular *corrie* or hollow, lies the Dwarfie Stone. It is a huge sandstone rock, of one solid stone, being about seven feet high, twenty-two feet long, and seventeen feet broad. The upper end of this stone is hewn into a sort of apartment containing two beds of stone and a passage between them. The uppermost and largest is five feet eight inches long, by two feet broad, and is furnished with a stone pillow. The lower supposed for the Dwarf's Wife, is shorter, and rounded off, instead of being square at the corners. The entrance may be about three feet and a half square. Before it lies a huge stone, apparently intended to serve the purpose of a door, and shaped accordingly. In the top, over the passage which divides the beds, there is a hole to serve for a window or chimney, which was doubtless originally wrought square with irons, like the rest of the work, but has been broken out by violence into a shapeless hole. Opposite to this stone, and proceeding from it in a line down the valley, are several small barrows, and there is a very large one on the same line, at the spot where we landed. This seems to indicate that the monument is of heathen times, and probably was meant as the temple of some northern edition of the *Dii Manes*. There are no symbols of Christian devotion — and the door is to the westward; it therefore does not seem to have been the abode of a hermit, as Dr. Barry[1] has conjectured. The Orcadians have no tradition on the subject, excepting that they believe it to be the work of a dwarf, to whom, like their ancestors, they attribute supernatural powers and

[1] History of the Orkney Islands, by the Rev. George Barry, D.D. 4to. Edinburgh : 1805.

malevolent disposition. They conceive he may be seen sometimes sitting at the door of his abode, but he vanishes on a nearer approach. Whoever inhabited this den certainly enjoyed

Pillow cold and sheets not warm.

Duff, Stevenson, and I, now walk along the skirts of the Hill of Hoy, to rejoin Robert Hamilton, who in the meanwhile had rode down to the clergyman's house, the wet and boggy walk not suiting his gout. Arrive at the manse completely wet, and drink tea there. The clergyman (Mr Hamilton) has procured some curious specimens of natural history for Bullock's Museum, particularly a pair of fine eaglets. He has just got another of the golden, or white kind, which he intends to send him. The eagle, with every other ravenous bird, abounds among the almost inaccessible precipices of Hoy, which afford them shelter, while the moors, abounding with grouse, and the small uninhabited islands and holms, where sheep and lambs are necessarily left unwatched, as well as the all-sustaining ocean, give these birds of prey the means of support. The clergyman told us that a man was very lately alive in the island of who, when an infant, was transported from thence by an eagle over a broad sound, or arm of the sea, to the bird's nest in Hoy. Pursuit being instantly made, and the eagle's nest being known, the infant was found there playing with the young eaglets. A more ludicrous instance of transportation he himself witnessed. Walking in the fields, he heard the squeaking of a pig for some time, without being able to discern whence it proceeded, until looking up, he beheld the unfortunate grunter in the talons of an eagle, who soared away with him towards the summit of Hoy. From this it may be conjectured that the island is very thinly inhabited in fact we only saw two or three little wigwams. After tea we walked a mile farther, to a point where the boat was lying, in order to secure the advantage of the flood-tide. We rowed with toil across one stream of tide, which set strongly up between Græmsay and Hoy; but, on turning the point of Græmsay, the other branch of the same flood-tide carried us with great velocity alongside our yacht, which we reached about nine o'clock. Between riding, walking, and running, we have spent a very active and entertaining day.

Domestic Memoranda. —The eggs on Zetland and Orkney are very indifferent, having an earthy taste, and being very small. But the hogs are an excellent breed — queer wild-looking creatures, with heads like wild-boars, but making capital bacon.

Off Stromness,17th August, 1814. — Went on shore after breakfast, and found W. Erskine and Marjoribanks had been in this town all last night, without our hearing of them or they of us. No letters from Abbotsford or Edinburgh. Stromness is a little dirty straggling town, which cannot be traversed by a cart, or even by a horse, for there are stairs up and down, even in the principal streets. We paraded its whole length like turkeys in a string, I suppose to satisfy ourselves that there was a worse town in the Orkneys than the metropolis, Kirkwall. We clomb, by steep and dirty lanes, an eminence rising above the town, and commanding a fine view. An old hag lives in a wretched cabin on this height, and subsists by selling winds. Each captain of a merchantman, between jest and earnest, gives the old woman sixpence, and she boils her kettle to procure a favourable gale. She was a miserable figure; upwards of ninety, she told us, and dried up like a mummy. A sort of clay-coloured cloak, folded over her head, corresponded in colour to her corpse like complexion. Fine light-blue eyes, and nose and chin that almost met, and a ghastly expression of cunning, gave her quite the effect of Hecate. She told us she remembered *Gow the pirate*, who was born near the House of Clestrom, and afterwards commenced buccaneer. He came to his native country about 1725, with a *snow* which he commanded, carried off two women from one of the islands, and committed other enormities. At length, while he was dining in a house in the island of Eda, the islanders, headed by Malcolm Laing's grandfather, made him prisoner, and sent him to London, where he was hanged. While at Stromness, he made love to a Miss Gordon, who pledged her faith to him by shaking hands, an engagement which, in her idea, could not be dissolved without her going to London to seek back again her "faith and troth," by shaking hands with him again after execution. We left our Pythoness, who assured us there was nothing evil in the intercession she was to make for us, but that we were only to have a fair wind through the benefit of her prayers. She repeated a sort of rigmarole which I suppose she had ready for such occasions, and seemed greatly delighted and surprised with the amount of our donations as everybody gave her a trifle, our faithful Captain Wilson making the regular offering on behalf of the ship. So much for buying a wind. Bessy Millie's habitation is airy enough for Æolus himself, but if she is a special favourite with that divinity, he has a strange choice. In her house I remarked a quern, or hand-mill. — A cairn, a little higher, commands a beautiful view of the bay, with its various entrances and islets. Here we found the vestiges of a bonfire, lighted in memory of the battle of Bannockburn, concerning which every part of Scotland has its peculiar traditions. The Orcadians say that a Norwegian prince, then their ruler, called by them Harold, brought 1400 men of Orkney to the assistance of Bruce, and that the King at a critical period of the engagement, touched him with his scabbard, saying, "The day is against us." — "I trust," returned the Orcadian, "your Grace will *venture again*"; which has given rise to their motto, and passed into a proverb. On board at half-past three, and find Bessy Millie a woman of her word, for the expected breeze has sprung up, if it but last us till we double Cape Wrath. Weigh anchor (I hope) to bid farewell to Orkney.[1]

The land in Orkney is, generally speaking, excellent, and what is not fitted for the plough is admirably adapted for pasture. But the cultivation is very bad, and the mode of using these extensive commons, where they tear up, without remorse, the turf of the finest pasture, in order to make fuel, is absolutely execrable. The practice has already peeled and exhausted much fine land, and must in the end ruin the country entirely. In other respects, their mode of cultivation is to manure for barley and oats, and then manure again, and this without the least idea of fallow or green crops. Mr. Rae thinks that his example — and he farms very well — has had no effect upon the natives, except in the article of potatoes, which they now cultivate a little more, but crops of turnips are unknown. For this slovenly labour the Orcadians cannot, like the Shetland men, plead the occupation of fishing, which is wholly neglected by them, excepting that about this time of the year all the people turn out for the dogfish, the liver of which affords oil, and the bodies are a food as much valued here by the lower classes as it is contemned in Shetland. We saw nineteen boats

[1]   Lord Teignmouth, in his recent 'Sketches of the Coasts and Islands of Scotland,' says 'The publication of the Pirate satisfied the natives of Orkney as to the authorship of the Waverley Novels. It was remarked by those who had accompanied Sir Walter Scott in his excursions in these Islands, that the vivid descriptions which the work contains were confined to those scenes which he visited.' - Vol. i.p. 28.

out at this work. But cod, tusk, ling, haddocks, etc., which abound round these isles, are totally neglected. Their inferiority in husbandry is therefore to be ascribed to the prejudices of the people, who are all peasants of the lowest order. On Lord Armadale's estate, the number of tenantry amounts to 300, and the average of rent is about seven pounds each. What can be expected from such a distribution? and how is the necessary restriction to take place, without the greatest immediate distress and hardship to these poor creatures? It is the hardest chapter in Economics; and if I were an Orcadian laird, I feel I should shuffle on with the old useless creatures, in contradiction to my better judgment. Stock is improved in these islands, and the horses seem to be better bred than in Shetland; at least, I have seen more clever animals. The good horses find a ready sale; Mr. Rae gets twenty guineas readily for a colt of his rearing — to be sure, they are very good.

Six o'Clock — Our breeze has carried us through the Mouth of Hoy, and so into the Atlantic. The north-western face of the island forms a ledge of high perpendicular cliffs, which might have surprised us more, had we not already seen the Ord of Bressay, the Noup of Noss, and the precipices of the Fair Isle. But these are formidable enough. One projecting cliff, from the peculiarities of its form, has acquired the name of the Old Man of Hoy, and is well known to mariners as marking the entrance to the Mouth. The other jaw of this mouth is formed by a lower range of crags, called the Burgh of Birsa. The access through this strait would be easy, — were it not for the Island of Græmsay, lying in the very throat of the passage, and two other islands covering the entrance to the harbour of Stromness. Græmsay is infamous for shipwrecks, and the chance of these *God-sends*, as they were impiously called, is said sometimes to have doubled the value of the land. In Stromness, I saw many of the sad relics of shipwrecked vessels applied to very odd purposes, and indeed to all sorts of occasions. The Gates, or *grinds*, as they are here called, are usually of ship planks and timbers, and so are their bridges, etc. These casualties are now much less common since the lights on the Skerries and the Start have been established. Enough of memoranda for the present. — We have hitherto kept our course pretty well; and a King's ship about eighteen guns or so, two miles upon our lee-boom, has shortened sail, apparently to take us under her wing, which may not be altogether unnecessary in the latitude of Cape Wrath, where several vessels have been taken by Yankee-Doodle. The sloop-of-war looks as if she could bite hard, and is supposed by our folks to be the Malay. If we can speak the captain, we will invite him to some grouse, or send him some, as he likes best, for Marchie's campaign was very successful.

18th August, 1814.— Bessy Millie's charm has failed us. After a rainy night, the wind has come round to the north-west, and is getting almost contrary. We have weathered Whitten-head, however, and Cape Wrath, the north-western extremity of Britain, is now in sight. The weather gets rainy and squally. Hamilton and Erskine keep their berths. Duff and I sit upon deck, like two great bears, wrapt in watch-cloaks, the sea flying over us every now and then. At length, after a sound buffeting with the rain, the doubling Cape Wrath with this wind is renounced as impracticable, and we stand away for Loch Eribol, a lake running into the extensive country of Lord Reay. No sickness; we begin to get hardy sailors in that particular. The ground rises upon us very bold and mountainous, especially a very high steep mountain, called Ben-y-Hope, at the head of a lake called Loch Hope. The weather begins to mitigate as we get under the lee of the land. Loch Eribol opens, running up into a wild and barren scene of crags and hills. The proper anchorage is said to be at the head of the lake, but to go eight miles up so narrow an inlet would expose us to be wind-bound. A pilot boat comes off from Mr. Anderson's house, a principal tacksman of Lord Reay's. After some discussion we anchor within a reef of sunken rocks, nearly opposite to Mr. Anderson's house of Rispan; the situation is not, we are given to understand, altogether without danger if the wind should blow hard, but it is now calm. In front of our anchorage a few shapeless patches of land, not exceeding a few yards in diameter, have been prepared for corn by the spade, and bear wretched crops. All the rest of the view is utter barrenness; the distant hills, we are told, contain plenty of deer, being part of a forest belonging to Lord Reay, who is proprietor of all the extensive range of desolation now under our eye. The water has been kinder than the land, for we hear of plenty of salmon, and haddocks, and lobsters, and send our faithful minister of the interior, John Peters, the steward, to procure some of those good things of this very indifferent land, and to invite Mr. Anderson to dine with us. Four o'clock, — John has just returned, successful in both commissions, and the evening concludes pleasantly.

19th August, 1814. Loch Eribol, near Cape Wrath. — Went off before eight a.m. to breakfast with our friend Mr. Anderson. His house invisible from the vessel at her moorings, and indeed, from any part of the entrance into Loch Eribol, is a very comfortable one, lying obscured behind a craggy eminence. A little creek, winding up behind the crag, and in front of the house, forms a small harbour, and gives a romantic air of concealment and snugness. There we found a ship upon the stocks, built from the keel by a Highland carpenter, who had magnanimously declined receiving assistance from any of the ship-carpenters who happened to be here occasionally, lest it should be said he could not have finished his task without their aid. An ample Highland breakfast of excellent new-taken herring, equal to those of Lochfine, fresh haddocks, fresh eggs, and fresh butter, not forgetting the bottle of whisky, and bannocks of barley, and oat-cakes, with the Lowland luxuries of tea and coffee. After breakfast, took the long-boat, and under Mr. Anderson's pilotage, row to see a remarkable natural curiosity, called Uamh Smowe, or the Largest Cave. Stevenson, Marchie, and Duff go by land. Take the fowling-piece, and shoot some sea-fowl and a large hawk of an uncommon appearance. Fire four shots, and kill three times. After rowing about three miles to the westward of the entrance from the sea to Loch Eribol, we enter a creek, between two ledges of very high rocks, and landing, find ourselves in front of the wonder we came to see. The exterior apartment of the cavern opens under a tremendous rock, facing the creek, and occupies the full space of the ravine where we landed. From the top of the rock to the base of the cavern, as we afterwards discovered by plumb, is eighty feet, of which the height of the arch is fifty-three feet: the rest, being twenty-seven feet, is occupied by the precipitous rock under which it opens; the width is fully in proportion to this great height, being 110 feet. The depth of this exterior cavern is 200 feet, and it is apparently supported by an intermediate column of natural rock. Being open to daylight and the sea air, the cavern is perfectly clean and dry, and the sides are incrusted with stalactites. This immense cavern is so well proportioned that I was not aware of its extraordinary height and extent till I saw our two friends, who had somewhat preceded us, having made the journey by land, appearing like pigmies among its recesses. Afterwards, on entering the cave, I climbed up a sloping rock at its extremity, and was much struck with the prospect, looking outward from this magnificent arched cavern upon our boat and its crew, the view being otherwise bounded by the ledge of rocks which formed each side of the creek. We now propose to investigate the farther wonders of the cave of Smowe. In the right or west side of the cave opens an interior cavern of a different aspect. The height of this second passage may be about twelve or fourteen feet, and its breadth about six or eight, neatly formed into a Gothic portal by the hand of nature. The lower part of this porch is closed by a ledge of rock, rising to the height of between five and six feet, and which I can compare to nothing but the hatch-door of a shop. Beneath this hatch a brook finds its way out, forms a black deep pool before the Gothic archway, and then escapes to the sea, and forms the creek in which we landed. It is somewhat difficult to approach this strange pass, so as to gain a view into the interior of the cavern. By clambering along a broken and dangerous cliff, you can, however, look into it; but only so far as to see a twilight space filled with dark-coloured water in great agitation, and representing a subterranean lake, moved by some fearful convulsion of nature. How this pond is supplied with water you cannot see from even this point of vantage, but you are made partly sensible of the truth by a sound like the dashing of a sullen cataract within the bowels of the earth. Here the adventure has usually been abandoned, and Mr. Anderson only mentioned two travellers whose curiosity had led them farther. We were resolved, however, to see the adventures of this new cave of Montesinos to an end. Duff had already secured the use of a fisher's boat and its hands, our own long-boat being too heavy and far too valuable to be ventured upon this Cocytus. Accordingly the skiff was dragged up the brook to the rocky ledge or hatch which barred up the interior cavern, and there, by force of hands, our boat's crew and two or three fishers first raised the boat's bow upon the ledge of rock, then brought her to a level, being poised upon that narrow hatch, and lastly launched her down into the dark and deep subterranean lake within. The entrance was so narrow, and the boat so clumsy, that we, who were all this while clinging to the rock like sea-fowl, and with scarce more secure footing, were greatly alarmed for the safety of our trusty sailors. At the instant when the boat sloped inward to the cave, a Highlander threw himself into it with great boldness and dexterity, and, at the expense of some bruises, shared its precipitate fall into the waters under the earth. This dangerous exploit was to prevent the boat drifting away from us, but a cord at its stern would have been a safer and surer expedient.

When our *enfant perdu* had recovered breath and legs, he brought the boat back to the entrance, and took us in. We now found ourselves embarked on a deep black pond of an irregular form, the rocks rising like a dome all around us, and high over our heads. The light, a sort of dubious twilight, was derived from two chasms in the roof of the vault, for that offered by the entrance was but trifling. Down one of those rents there poured from the height of eighty feet, in a sheet of foam, the brook, which, after supplying the subterranean pond with water, finds its way out beneath the ledge of rock that blocks its entrance. The other skylight, if I may so term it, looks out at the clear blue sky. It is impossible for description to explain the impression made by so strange a place, to which we had been conveyed with so much difficulty. The cave itself, the pool, the cataract, would have been each separate objects of wonder, but all united together, and affecting at once the ear, the eye, and the imagination, their effect is indescribable. The length of this pond, or loch, as the people here call it, is seventy feet over, the breadth about thirty at the narrowest point, and it is of great depth.

As we resolved to proceed, we directed the boat to a natural arch on the right hand, or west side of the cataract. This archway was double, a high arch being placed above a very low one, as in a Roman aqueduct. The ledge of rock which forms this lower arch is not above two feet and a half high above the water, and under this we were to pass in the boat; so that we were fain to pile ourselves flat upon each other like a layer of herrings. By this judicious disposition we were pushed in safety beneath this low-browed rock into a region of utter darkness. For this, however, we were provided, for we had a tinder-box and lights. The view back upon the twilight lake we had crossed, its sullen eddies wheeling round and round, and its echoes resounding

Smowe Cave

to the ceaseless thunder of the waterfall, seemed dismal enough, and was aggravated by temporary darkness, and in some degree by a sense of danger. The lights, however, dispelled the latter sensation, if it prevailed to any extent, and we now found ourselves in a narrow cavern, sloping somewhat upward from the water. We got out of the boat, proceeded along some slippery places upon shelves of the rock, and gained the dry land. I cannot say *dry*, excepting comparatively. We were then in an arched cave, twelve feet high in the roof, and about eight feet in breadth, which went winding into the bowels of the earth for about an hundred feet. The sides, being (like those of the whole cavern) of limestone rock, were covered with stalactites, and with small drops of water like dew, glancing like ten thousand thousand sets of birthday diamonds under the glare of our lights. In some places these stalactites branch out into broad and curious ramifications, resembling coral and the foliage of submarine plants.

When we reached the extremity of this passage, we found it declined suddenly to a horrible ugly gulf, or well, filled with dark water, and of great depth, over which the rock closed. We threw in stones, which indicated great profundity by their sound; and growing more familiar with the horrors of this den, we sounded with an oar, and found about ten feet depth at the entrance, but discovered in the same manner that the gulf extended under the rock, deepening as it went, God knows how far. Imagination can figure few deaths more horrible than to be sucked under these rocks into some unfathomable abyss, where your corpse could never be found to give intimation of your fate. A water kelpie, or an evil spirit of any aquatic propensities, could not choose a fitter abode; and, to say the truth, I believe at our first entrance, and when all our feelings were afloat at the novelty of the scene, the unexpected plashing of a seal would have routed the whole dozen of us. The mouth of this ugly gulf was all covered with slimy alluvious substances, which led Mr. Stevenson to observe that it could have no separate source, but must be fed from the waters of the outer lake and brook, as it lay upon the same level, and seemed to rise and fall with them, without having anything to indicate a separate current of its own. Rounding this perilous hole, or gulf, upon the aforesaid alluvious substances, which formed its shores, we reached the extremity of the cavern, which there ascends like a vent, or funnel, directly up a sloping precipice, but hideously black and slippery from wet and seaweeds. One of our sailors, a Zetlander, climbed up a good way, and by holding up a light, we could plainly perceive that this vent closed after ascending to a considerable height; and here, therefore, closed the adventure of the cave of Smowe, for it appeared utterly impossible to proceed further in any direction whatever. There is a tradition that the first Lord Reay went through various subterranean abysses, and at length returned, after ineffectually endeavouring to penetrate to the extremity of the Smowe cave; but this must be either fabulous, or an exaggerated account of such a journey as we performed. And under the latter supposition, it is a curious instance how little the people in the neighbourhood of this curiosity have cared to examine it.

In returning, we endeavoured to familiarize ourselves with the objects in detail, which, viewed together, had struck us with so much wonder. The stalactites, or limy incrustations, upon the walls of the cavern, are chiefly of a dark-brown colour, and in this respect Smowe is inferior, according to Mr. Stevenson, to the celebrated cave of Macallister in the Isle of Skye. In returning, the men with the lights, and the various groups and attitudes of the party, gave a good deal of amusement. We now ventured to clamber along the side of the rock above the subterranean water, and thus gained the upper arch, and had the satisfaction to see our admirable and good-humoured Commodore, Hamilton, floated beneath the lower arch into the second cavern. His goodly countenance being illumined by a single candle, his recumbent posture, and the appearance of a hard-favoured fellow guiding the boat, made him the very picture of Bibo, in the catch, when he wakes in Charon's boat :

> When Bibo thought fit from this world to retreat,
> As full of Champagne as an egg's full of meat,
> He waked in the boat, and to Charon he said,
> That he would be row'd back, for he was not yet dead.

Descending from our superior station on the upper arch, we now again embarked, and spent some time in rowing about and examining this second cave. We could see our dusky entrance, into which daylight streamed faint, and at a considerable distance; and under the arch of the outer cavern stood a sailor, with an oar in his hand, looking, in the perspective, like a fairy with his wand. We at length emerged unwillingly from this extraordinary basin, and again enjoyed ourselves in the large exterior cave. Our boat was hoisted with some difficulty over the ledge, which appears the natural barrier of the interior apartments, and restored in safety to the fishers, who were properly gratified for the hazard which their skiff, as well as one of themselves, had endured. After this we resolved to ascend the rocks, and discover the opening by which the cascade was discharged from above into the second cave. Erskine and I, by some chance, took the wrong side of the rocks, and, after some scrambling, got into the face of a dangerous precipice, where Erskine, to my great alarm, turned giddy, and declared he could not go farther. I clambered up without much difficulty, and shouting to the people below, got two of them to assist the Counsellor, who was brought into, by the means which have sent many a good fellow out of, the world — I mean a rope. We easily found the brook, and traced its descent till it precipitates itself down a chasm of the rock into the subterranean apartment, where we first made its acquaintance. Divided by a natural arch of stone from the chasm down which the cascade falls, there is another rent, which serves as a skylight to the cavern, as I already noticed. Standing on a natural foot-bridge, formed by the arch which divides these two gulfs, you have a grand prospect into both. The one is deep, black, and silent, only affording at the bottom a glimpse of the dark and sullen pool which occupies the interior of the cavern. The right-hand rent, down which the stream discharges itself, seems to ring and reel with the unceasing roar of the cataract which envelopes its side in mist and foam. This part of the scene alone is worth a day's journey. After heavy rains, the torrent is discharged into this cavern with astonishing violence; and the size of the chasm being inadequate to the reception of such a volume of water, it is thrown up in spouts like the blowing of a whale. But at such times the entrance of the cavern is inaccessible.

Taking leave of this scene with regret, we rowed back to Loch Eribol. Having yet an hour to spare before dinner, we rowed across the mouth of the lake to its shore on the east side. This rises into a steep and shattered stack of mouldering calcareous rock and stone, called Whiten-head. It is pierced with several caverns, the abode of seals and cormorants. We entered one, where our guide promised to us a grand sight, and so it certainly would have been to any who had not just come from Smowe. In this last cave the sea enters through a lofty arch, and penetrates to a great depth; but the weight of the tide made it dangerous to venture very far, so we did not see the extremity of Friskin's Cavern as it is called. We shot several cormorants in the cave, the echoes roaring like thunder at every discharge. We received, however, a proper rebuke from Hamilton, our commodore, for killing anything which was not fit for *eating*. It was in vain I assured him that the Zetlanders made excellent hare-soup out of these sea-fowl. He will listen to no subordinate authority, and rules us by the Almanach des Gourmands. Mr. Anderson showed me the spot where the Norwegian monarch, Haco, moored his fleet, after the discomfiture he received at Largs. He caused all the cattle to be driven from the hills, and houghed and slain upon a broad flat rock, for the refreshment of his dispirited army. Mr. Anderson dines with us, and very handsomely presents us with a stock of salmon, haddocks, and so forth, which we requite by a small present of wine from our sea stores. This has been a fine day; the first fair day here for these eight weeks.

20th August, 1814. — Sail by four in the morning, and by half-past six are off Cape Wrath. All hands ashore by seven, and no time allowed to breakfast, except on beef and biscuit. On this dread Cape, so fatal to mariners, it is proposed to build a lighthouse, and Mr. Stevenson has fixed on an advantageous situation. It is a high promontory, with steep sides that go sheer down to the breakers, which lash its feet. There is no landing, except in a small creek about a mile and a half to the eastward. There the foam of the sea plays at long bowls with a huge collection of large stones, some of them a ton in weight, but which these fearful billows chuck up and down as a child tosses a ball. The walk from thence to the Cape was over rough boggy ground, but good sheep pasture. Mr. — Dunlop, brother to the laird of Dunlop, took from Lord Reay, some years since a large track of sheep-land, including the territories of Cape Wrath, for about £300 a year, for the period of two-nineteen years and a life-rent. It is needless to say that the tenant has an immense profit, for the value of pasture is now understood here. Lord Reay's estate, containing 150,000 square acres, and measuring eighty miles by sixty, was, before commencement of the last leases, rented at £1200 a year. It is now worth £5000, and

Mr. Anderson says he may let it this ensuing year (when the leases expire) for about £15,000. But then he must resolve to part with his people, for these rents can only be given upon the supposition that sheep are generally to be introduced on the property. In an economical, and perhaps in a political point of view, it might be best that every part of a country were dedicated to that sort of occupation for which nature has best fitted it. But to effect this reform in the present instance, Lord Reay must turn out several hundred families who have lived under him and his fathers for many generations, and the swords of whose fathers probably won the lands from which he is now expelling them. He is a good-natured man, I suppose, for Mr. A. says he is hesitating whether he shall not take a more moderate rise (£7000 or £8000), and keep his Highland tenantry. This last war (before the short peace), he levied a fine fencible corps (the Reay fencibles), and might have doubled their number. *Wealth* is no doubt *strength* in a country, while all is quiet and governed by law, but on any altercation or internal commotion, it ceases to be strength, and is only the means of tempting the strong to plunder the possessors. Much may be said on both sides.[1]

Cape Wrath is a striking point, both from the dignity of its own appearance, and from the mental association of its being the extreme cape of Scotland, with reference to the north-west. There is no land in the direct line between this point and America. I saw a pair of large eagles, and if I had had the rifle-gun might have had a shot, for the birds, when I first saw them, were perched on a rock within about sixty or seventy yards. They are, I suppose, little disturbed here, for they showed no great alarm. After the Commissioners and Mr. Stevenson had examined the headland, with reference to the site of a lighthouse, we strolled to our boat, and came on board between ten and eleven. Get the boat up upon deck, and set sail for the Lewis with light winds and a great swell of tide. Pass a rocky islet called Gousla. Here a fine vessel was lately wrecked; all her crew perished but one, who got upon the rocks from the boltsprit, and was afterwards brought off. In front of Cape Wrath are some angry breakers, called the *Staggs*;

---

[1]   The whole of the immense district called Lord Reay's country the habitation, as far back as history reaches, of the clan Mackay-has passed, since Sir W. Scott's journal was written, into the hands of the noble family of Sutherland.

the rocks which occasion them are visible at low water. The country behind Cape Wrath swells in high sweeping elevations, but without any picturesque or dignified mountainous scenery. But on sailing westward a few miles, particularly after doubling a headland called the Stour of Assint, the coast assumes the true Highland character, being skirted with a succession of picturesque mountains of every variety of height and outline. These are the hills of Ross-shire — a waste and thinly-peopled district at this extremity of the island. We would willingly have learned the names of the most remarkable, but they are only laid down in the charts by the cant names given them by mariners, from their appearance, as the Sugar-loaf, and so forth. Our breeze now increases, and seems steadily favourable, carrying us on with exhilarating rapidity, at the rate of eight knots an hour, with the romantic outline of the mainland under our lee-beam, and the dusky shores of the Long Island beginning to appear ahead. We remain on deck long after it is dark, watching the phosphoric effects occasioned, or made visible, by the rapid motion of the vessel, and enlightening her course with a continued succession of sparks and even flashes of broad light, mingled with the foam which she flings from her bows and head. A rizard haddock and to bed. Charming weather all day.

21st August, 1814. — Last night went out like a lamb, but this morning came in like a lion, all roar and tumult. The wind shifted and became squally; the mingled and confused tides that run among the Hebrides got us among their eddies, and gave the cutter such concussions, that, besides reeling at every wave, she trembled from head to stern, with a sort of very uncomfortable and ominous vibration. Turned out about three, and went on deck the prospect dreary enough, as we are beating up a narrow channel between two dark and disconsolate — looking islands, in a gale of wind and rain, guided only by the twinkling glimmer of the light on an island called Ellan Glas — Go to bed and sleep soundly, notwithstanding the rough rocking. Great bustle about four; the lightkeeper having seen our flag, comes off to be our pilot, as in duty bound. Asleep again till eight. When I went on deck, I found we had anchored in the little harbour of Scalpa, upon the coast of Harris, a place dignified by the residence of Charles Edward in his hazardous attempt to escape in 1746. An old man, lately alive here, called Donald Macleod, was his host and temporary protector, and could not, until his dying hour, mention the distresses of the adventurer without tears. From this place, Charles attempted to go to Stornoway; but the people of the Lewis had taken arms to secure him, under an idea that he was coming to plunder the country. And although his faithful attendant, Donald Macleod, induced them by fair words to lay aside their purpose, yet they insisted upon his leaving the island. So the unfortunate Prince was obliged to return back to Scalpa. He afterwards escaped to South Uist, but was chased in the passage by Captain Fergusson's sloop of war. The harbour seems a little neat secure place of anchorage. Within a small island, there seems more shelter than where we are lying but it is crowded with vessels, part of those whom we saw in the Long-Hope — so Mr. Wilson chose to remain outside. The ground looks hilly and barren in the extreme; but I can say little for it, as an incessant rain prevents my keeping the deck. Stevenson and Duff, accompanied by Marchie go to examine the lighthouse on Ellan Glas. Hamilton and Erskine keep their beds, having scarce slept last night — and I bring up my journal. The day continues bad, with little intermission of rain. Our party return with little advantage from their expedition, excepting some fresh butter from the lighthouse. The harbour of Scalpa is composed of a great number of little uninhabited islets. The masts of the vessels at anchor behind them have a good effect. To bed early, to make amends for last night, with the purpose of sailing for Dunvegan in the Isle of Skye with daylight.

22nd August, 1814. — Sailed early in the morning from Scalpa Harbour, in order to cross the Minch, or Channel, for Dunvegan; but the breeze being contrary, we can only creep along the Harris shore, until we shall gain the advantage of the tide. The east coast of Harris, as we now see it, is of a character which sets human industry at utter defiance, consisting of high sterile hills, covered entirely with stones, with a very slight sprinkling of stunted heather. Within, appear still higher peaks of mountains. I have never seen anything more unpropitious, excepting the southern side of Griban, on the shores of Loch-na-Gaoil, in the Isle of Mull. We sail along this desolate coast (which exhibits no mark of human habitation) with the advantage of a pleasant day, and a brisk though not a favourable gale. *Two o'clock* — Row ashore to see the little harbour and village of Rowdill, on the

The Lighthouse, Scalpa

coast of Harris. There is a decent three-storied house, belonging to the laird, Mr. Macleod of the Harris,[1] where we were told two of his female relations lived. A large vessel had been stranded last year, and two or three carpenters were about repairing her, but in such a style of Highland laziness that I suppose she may float next century. The harbour is neat enough, but wants a little more cover to the eastward. The ground, on landing, does not seem altogether so desolate as from the sea. In the former point of view, we overlook all the retired glens and crevices, which, by infinite address and labour, are rendered capable of a little cultivation. But few and evil are the patches so cultivated in Harris, as far as we have seen. Above the house is situated the ancient church of Rowdill. This pile was unfortunately burned down by accident some years since, by fire taking to a quantity of wood laid in for fitting it up. It is a building in the form of a cross, with a rude tower at the eastern end, like some old English churches. Upon this tower are certain pieces of sculpture, of a kind the last which one would have expected on a building dedicated to religious purposes. Some have lately fallen in a storm, but enough remains to astonish us at the grossness of the architect and the age.

Within the church are two ancient monuments. The first, on the right hand of the pulpit, presents the effigy of a warrior completely armed in plate armour, with his hand on his two-handed broadsword. His helmet is peaked, with a gorget or upper corslet which seems to be made of mail. His figure lies flat on the monument, and is in bas-relief, of the natural size. The arch which surmounts this monument is curiously carved with the figures of the apostles. In the flat space of the wall beneath the arch, and above the tombstone, are a variety of compartments, exhibiting the arms of the MacLeods, being a galley with the sails spread, a rude view of Dunvegan Castle, some saints and religious emblems, and a Latin inscription, of which our time (or skill) was inadequate to decipher the first line; but the others announced the tenant of the monument to be *Alexander, filius Willielmi MacLeod, de Dunvegan, Anno Dni* M.CCCC.XXVIII. A much older monument (said also to represent a Laird of MacLeod) lies in the transept, but without any arch over it. It represents the grim figure of a Highalnd chief, not in feudal armour like the former, but dressed in

---

[1]   The Harris has recently passed into the possession of the Earl of Dunmore. - [1839.]

a plaid — (or perhaps a shirt of mail) — reaching down below the knees, with a broad sort of hem upon its lower extremity. The figure wears a high-peaked open helmet, or skull-cap, with a sort of tippet of mail attached to it, which falls over the breast of the warrior, pretty much as women wear a handkerchief or short shawl. This remarkable figure is bearded most tyrannically, and has one hand on his long two-handed sword, the other on his dirk, both of which hang at a broad belt. Another weapon, probably his knife, seems to have been also attached to the baldric. His feet rest on his two dogs entwined together, and a similar emblem is said to have supported his head, but is now defaced, as indeed the whole monument bears marks of the unfortunate fire. A lion is placed at each end of the stone. Who the hero was, whom this martial monument commemorated, we could not learn. Indeed, our Cicerone was but imperfect. He chanced to be a poor devil of an excise-officer who had lately made a seizure of a still upon a neighbouring island, after a desperate resistance. Upon seeing our cutter, he mistook it, as has often happened to us, for an armed vessel belonging to the revenue, which the appearance and equipment of the yacht, and the number of men, make her resemble considerably. He was much disappointed when he found we had nothing to do with the tribute to Cæsar, and begged us not to undeceive the natives, who were so much irritated against him that he found it necessary to wear a loaded pair of pistols in each pocket, which he showed to our Master, Wilson, to convince him of the perilous state in which he found himself while exercising so obnoxious a duty in the midst of a fierce-tempered people, and at many miles distance from any possible countenance or assistance. The village of Rowdill consists of Highland huts of the common construction, *i.e.* a low circular wall of large stones, without mortar, deeply sunk in the ground, surmounted by a thatched roof secured by ropes, without any chimney but a hole in the roof. There may be forty such houses in the village. We heard that the laird was procuring a schoolmaster — he of the parish being ten miles distant — and there was a neatness about the large house which seems to indicate that things are going on well. Adjacent to the churchyard were two eminences, apparently artificial. Upon one was fixed a stone, seemingly the staff of a cross; upon another the head of a cross, with a sculpture of the crucifixion. These monuments (which refer themselves to Catholic times of course) are popularly called *The Croshlets* — crosslets, or little crosses.

Get on board at five, and stand across the Sound for Skye with the ebb-tide in our favour. The sunset being delightful, we enjoy it upon deck, admiring the Sound on each side bounded by islands. That of Skye lies in the east, with some very high mountains in the centre, and a bold rocky coast in front, opening up into several lochs, or arms of the sea; — that of Loch Folliart, near the upper end of which Dunvegan is situated, is opposite to us, but our breeze has failed us, and the flood-tide will soon set in, which is likely to carry us to the northward of this object of our curiosity until next morning. To the west of us lies Harris, with its variegated ridges of mountains, now clear, distinct, and free from clouds. The sun is just setting behind the Island of Bernera, of which we see one conical hill. North Uist and Benbecula continue from Harris to the southerly line of what is called the Long Island. They are as bold and mountainous, and probably as barren as Harris — worse they cannot be. Unnumbered islets and holms, each of which has its name and its history, skirt these larger isles, and are visible in this clear evening as distinct and separate objects, lying lone and quiet upon the face of the undisturbed and scarce-rippling sea. To our berths at ten, after admiring the scenery for some time.

23rd August, 1814. — Wake under the Castle of Dunvegan, in the Loch of Folliart. I had sent a card to the Laird of Macleod in the morning, who came off before we were dressed, and carried us to his castle to breakfast. A part of Dunvegan is very old; "its birth tradition notes not." Another large tower was built by the same Alaster Macleod whose burial-place and monument we saw yesterday at Rowdill. He had a Gaelic surname, signifying the Hump-backed. Roderick More (knighted by James VI.) erected a long edifice combining these two ancient towers: and other pieces of building, forming a square, were accomplished at different times. The whole castle occupies a precipitous mass of rock overhanging the lake, divided by two or three islands in that place, which form a snug little harbour under the walls. There is a courtyard looking out upon the sea, protected by a battery, at least a succession of embrasures, for only two guns are pointed, and these unfit for service. The ancient entrance rose up a flight of steps cut in the rock, and passed into this courtyard through a portal, but this is now demolished. You land under the castle, and walking round, find

Dunvegan Castle

yourself in front of it. This was originally inaccessible, for a brook coming down on the one side, a chasm of the rocks on the other, and a ditch in front, made it impervious. But the late Macleod built a bridge over the stream, and the present laird is executing an entrance suitable to the character of this remarkable fortalice, by making a portal between two advanced towers and an outer court, from which he proposes to throw a drawbridge over to the high rock in front of the castle. This, if well executed, cannot fail to have a good and characteristic effect. We were most kindly and hospitably received by the chieftain, his lady, and his sister;[1] the two last are pretty and accomplished young women, a sort of persons whom we have not seen for some time; and I was quite as much pleased with renewing my acquaintance with them as with the sight of a good field of barley just cut (the first harvest we have seen), not to mention an extensive young plantation and some middle-aged trees, though all had been strangers to mine eyes since I left Leith. In the garden — or rather the orchard which was formerly the garden — is a pretty cascade, divided into two branches, and called Rorie More's Nurse, because he loved to be lulled to sleep by the sound of it. The day was rainy, or at least inconstant, so we could not walk far from the castle. Besides the assistance of the laird himself, who was most politely and easily attentive, we had that of an intelligent gentlemanlike clergyman, Mr. Suter, minister of Kilmore, to explain the *carte-de-pays*. Within the castle we saw a remarkable drinking-cup, with an inscription dated A.D.993, which I have described particularly elsewhere.[2] I saw also a fairy flag, a pennon of silk, with something like round red rowan-berries wrought upon it. We also saw the drinking-horn of Rorie More, holding about three pints English measure — an ox's horn tipped with silver, not nearly so large as Watt of Harden's bugle. The rest of the curiosities in the castle are chiefly Indian, excepting an old dirk and the fragment of a two-handed sword. We learn that most of the Highland superstitions, even that of the second-sight, are still in force. Gruagach, a sort of tutelary divinity, often mentioned by Martin in his history of the Western Islands, has still his place and credit, but is modernized into a tall man, always a Lowlander, with a long coat

[1]   Miss Macleod, now Mrs. Spencer Perceval.
[2]   See Note, Lord of the Isles, Scott's Poetical Works, vol. xp.294

and white waistcoat. Passed a very pleasant day. I should have said the fairy-flag had three properties. Produced in battle, it multiplied the numbers of the Macleods — spread on the nuptial bed, it ensured fertility — and lastly, it brought herring into the loch.[1]

24th August, 1814. — This morning resist with difficulty Macleod's kind and pressing entreaty to send round the ship, and go to the cave at Airds by land; but our party is too large to be accommodated without inconvenience, and divisions are always awkward. Walk and see Macleod's farm. The plantations seem to thrive admirably, although I think he hazards planting his trees greatly too tall. Macleod is a spirited and judicious improver, and if he does not hurry too fast, cannot fail to be of service to his people. He seems to think and act much like a chief, without the fanfaronade of the character. See a female

---

[1] The following passage, from the last of Scott's Letters on Demonology (written in 1830), refers to the night of this 23rd of August 1814. He mentions that twice in his life he had experienced the sensation which the Scotch call *eerie*; gives a night-piece of his early youth in the castle of Glammis, which has already been quoted (*ante*, vol. i. p. 186), and proceeds thus:- 'Amid such tales of ancient tradition, I had from Macleod and his lady the courteous offer of the the haunted apartment of the castle, about which, as a stranger, I might be supposed interested. Accordingly I took possession of it about the witching hour. Except, perhaps, some tapestry hangings, and the extreme thickness of the walls, which argued great antiquity, nothing could have been more comfortable than the interior of the apartment; but if you looked from the windows, the view was such as to correspond with the highest tone of superstition. An autumnal blast, sometimes clear, sometimes driving mist before it, swept along the troubled billows of the lake, which it occasionally concealed, and by fits disclosed.

The waves rushed in wild disorder on the shore, and covered with foam the steep pile of rocks, which, rising from the sea in forms something resembling the human figure, have obtained the name of Macleod's Maidens, and, in such a night, seemed no bad representative of the Norwegian goddesses, called Choosers of the Slain, or Riders of the Storm. There was something of the dignity of danger in the scene, for, on a platform beneath the windows, lay an ancient battery of cannon, which had sometimes been used against privateers even of late years. The distant scene was a view of that part of the Quillen mountains which are called, from their form, Macleod's Dining-Tables. The voice of an angry cascade, termed the Nurse of Rorie Mhor, because that chief slept best in its vicinity, was heard from time to time mingling its notes with those of wind and wave. Such was the haunted room at Dunvegan; and, as such, it well deserved a less sleepy inhabitant. In the language of Dr. Johnson, who has stamped his memory on this remote place, - "I looked around me, and wondered that I was not more affected; but the mind is not at all times equally ready to be moved." In a word, it is necessary to confess that, of all I heard or saw, the most engaging spectacle was the comfortable bed in which I hoped to make amends for some rough nights on shipboard, and where I slept accordingly without thinking of ghost or goblin, till I was called by my servant in the morning.'

school patronised by Mrs. M. There are about twenty girls, who learn reading, writing, and spinning; and being compelled to observe habits of cleanliness and neatness when at school, will, probably be the means of introducing them by degrees at home. The roads around the castle are, generally speaking, very good; some are old, some made under the operation of the late act. Macleod says almost all the contractors for these last roads have failed, being tightly looked after by Government, which I confess I think very right. If Government is to give relief where a disadvantageous contract has been engaged in, it is plain it cannot be refused in similar instances, so that all calculations of expenses in such operations are at an end. The day being delightfully fair and warm, we walk up to the Church of Kilmore. In a cottage, at no great distance, we heard the women singing as they *waulked* the cloth, by rubbing it with their hands and feet, and screaming all the while in a sort of chorus. At a distance, the sound was wild and sweet enough, but rather discordant when you approached too near the performers. In the churchyard (otherwise not remarkable) was a pyramidical monument erected to the father of the celebrated Simon, Lord Lovat, who was fostered at Dunvegan. It is now nearly ruinous, and the inscription has fallen down. Return to the castle, take our luncheon, and, go aboard at three — Macleod accompanying us in proper style with his piper. We take leave of the castle, where we have been so kindly entertained, with a salute of seven guns. The chief returns ashore, with his piper playing "the Macleod's gathering," heard to advantage along the calm and placid loch, and dying as it retreated from us.

The towers of Dunvegan, with the banner which floated over them in honour of their guests, now showed to great advantage. On the right were a succession of three remarkable hills, with round flat tops, popularly called Macleod's Dining-Tables. Far behind these, in the interior of the island, arise the much higher and more romantic mountains called Quillen, or Cuillin, a name which they have been said to owe to no less a person than Cuthullin, or Cuchullin, celebrated by Ossian. I ought, I believe, to notice that Macleod and Mr. Suter have both heard a tacksman of Macleod's, called Grant, recite the celebrated Address to the Sun; and another person, whom they named, repeat the description of Cuchullin's car. But all agree as to the gross infidelity of Macpherson as a translator and editor. It ends in the explanation of the Adventures in the cave of Montesinos, afforded to the Knight of La Mancha, by the ape of Gines de Passamonte — some are true and some are false. There is little poetical tradition in this country, yet there should be a great deal, considering how lately the bards and genealogists existed as a distinct order. Macleod's *hereditary* piper is called MacCrimmon, but the present holder of the office has risen above his profession. He is an old man, a lieutenant in the army, and a most capital piper, possessing about 200 tunes and pibrochs, most of which will probably die with him, as he declines to have any of his sons instructed in his art. He plays to Macleod and his lady, but only in the same room, and maintains his minstrel privilege by putting on his bonnet as soon as he begins to play. These MacCrimmons formerly kept a college in Skye for teaching the pipe-music. Macleod's present piper is of the name, but scarcely as yet a deacon of his craft. He played every day at dinner. — After losing sight of the Castle of Dunvegan, we open another branch of the loch on which it is situated, and see a small village upon its distant bank. The mountains of Quillen continue to form a background to the wild landscape with their variegated and peaked outlines. We approach Dunvegan-head, a bold bluff cape where the loch joins the ocean. The weather, hitherto so beautiful that we had dined on deck *en seigneurs*, becomes overcast and hazy, with little or no wind. Laugh and lie down.

25th August, 1814. — Rise about eight o'clock, the yacht gliding delightfully along the coast of Skye with a fair wind and excellent day. On the opposite side lie the islands of Canna, Rum, and Muick, popularly Muck. On opening the sound between Rum and Canna, see a steep circular rock, forming one side of the harbour, on the point of which we can discern the remains of a tower of small dimensions, built, it is said, by a King of the Isles to secure a wife of whom he was jealous. But, as we kept the Skye side of the Sound, we saw little of these islands but what our spy-glasses could show us. The coast of Skye is highly romantic, and at the same time displayed a richness of vegetation on the lower grounds, to which we have hitherto been strangers. We passed three salt-water lochs, or deep embayments, called Loch Bracadale, Loch Eynort, and Loch Britta — and about eleven o'clock open Loch Scavig. We were now under the western termination of the high mountains of Quillen, whose weather-beaten and serrated peaks we had admired at a distance from Dunvegan. They sunk here upon the sea, but with the same bold and peremptory aspect which their distant appearance indicated. They seemed to consist of precipitous sheets of naked rock, down which the torrents were leaping in a hundred lines of foam. The tops, apparently inaccessible to human foot, were rent and split into the most tremendous pinnacles; towards the base of these bare and precipitous crags, the ground, enriched by the soil washed away from them, is verdant and productive. Having passed within the small isle of Soa, we enter Loch Scavig under the shoulder of one of these grisly mountains, and observe that the opposite side of the loch is of a milder character softened down into steep green declivities. From the depth of the bay advanced a headland of high rocks which divided the lake into two recesses, from each of which a brook seemed to issue. Here Macleod had intimated we should find a fine romantic loch, but we were uncertain up what inlet we should proceed in search of it. We chose, against our better judgment, the southerly inlet, where we saw a house which might afford us information. On manning our boat and rowing ashore, we observed a hurry among the inhabitants, owing to our being as usual suspected for *king's men*, although, Heaven knows, we have nothing to do with the revenue but to spend the part of it corresponding to our equipment. We find that there is a lake adjoining to each branch of the bay, and foolishly walk a couple of miles to see that next the farmhouse, merely because the honest man seemed jealous of the honour of his own loch, though we were speedily convinced it was not that which we had been recommended to examine. It had no peculiar merit excepting from its neighbourhood to a very high cliff or mountain of precipitous granite; otherwise, the sheet of water does not equal even Cauldshiels Loch. Returned and re-embarked in our boat, for our guide shook his head at our proposal to climb over the peninsula which divides the two bays and the two lakes. In rowing round the headland, surprised at the infinite number of sea-fowl, then busy apparently with a shoal of fish; at the depth of the bay, find that the discharge from this second lake forms a sort of waterfall or rather rapid; round this place were assembled hundreds of trouts and salmon struggling to get up into the fresh water; with a net we might have had twenty salmon at a haul, and a sailor, with no better hook than a crooked pin, caught a dish of trouts during our absence.

Advancing up this huddling and riotous brook, we found ourselves in a most extraordinary scene: we were surrounded by hills of the boldest and most precipitous character, and on the margin of a lake which seemed to have sustained the constant ravages of torrents from these rude neighbours. The shores consisted of huge layers of naked granite, here and there intermixed with bogs and heaps of gravel and sand marking the course of torrents. Vegetation there was little or none, and the mountains rose so perpendicularly from the water's edge that Borrowdale is a jest to them. We proceeded about one mile and a half up this deep, dark, and solitary lake, which is about two miles long, half a mile broad, and, as we learned, of extreme depth. The vapour which enveloped the mountain ridges obliged us by assuming a thousand shapes, varying its veils in all sorts of forms, but sometimes clearing off altogether. It is true it made us pay the penalty by some heavy and downright showers, from the frequency of which, a Highland boy, whom we brought from the farm, told us the lake was popularly called the Water Kettle. The proper name is Loch Corriskin, from the deep *corrie* or hollow in the mountains of Cuillin, which affords the basin for this wonderful sheet of water. It is as exquisite as a savage scene, as Loch Katrine is as a scene of stern beauty. After having penetrated so far as distinctly to observe the termination of the lake, under an immense mountain which rises abruptly from the head of the waters, we returned, and often stopped to admire the ravages which storms must have made in these recesses when all human witnesses were driven to places of more shelter and security. Stones, or rather large massive fragments of rock of a composite kind, perfectly different from the granite barriers of the lake, lay upon the rocky beach in the strangest and most precarious situations, as if abandoned by the torrents which had borne them down from above; some lay loose and tottering upon the ledges of the natural rock, with so little security that the slightest push moved them, though their weight exceeded many tons. These detached rocks were chiefly what are called plum-pudding stones. Those which formed the shore were granite. The opposite side of the lake seemed quite pathless, as a huge mountain, one of the detached ridges of the Quillen, sinks in a profound and almost perpendicular precipice down to the water. On the left-hand side, which we traversed, rose a higher and equally inaccessible mountain, the top of which seemed to contain the crater of an exhausted volcano. I never saw a spot on which there was less appearance of vegetation of any kind; the eye rested on nothing but brown and naked crags,[1] and the rocks on which we walked by the side of the loch were as bare as the pavement of Cheapside. There are one or two spots of islets in the loch which seem to bear juniper, or some such low bushy shrub.

Returned from our extraordinary walk and went on board. During dinner, our vessel quitted Loch Scavig, and having doubled its southern cape, opened the bay or salt-water Loch of Sleapin. There went again on shore to visit the late discovered and much celebrated cavern called Macallister's Cave. It opens at the end of a deep ravine running upward from the sea, and the proprietor, Mr. Macallister of

---

[1]
Rarely human eye has known
A scene so stern as that dread lake,
With its dark ledge of barren stone.
Seems that primeval earthquake's sway
Hath rent a strange and shatter'd way
Through the rude bosom of the hill,
And that each naked precipice
Sable ravine, and dark abyss,
Tells of the outrage still.
The wildest glen, but this, can show
Some touch of Nature's genial glow
On high Benmore green mosses grow,
And heath-bells bud in deep Glencroe,
And copse on Cruchan-Ben;
But here-above, around, below,
On mountain or in glen,
Nor tree, nor shrub, nor plant, nor flower,
Nor aught of vegetative power,
The weary eye may ken;
For all is rocks at random thrown,
Black waves, bare crags, and banks of stone,
As if were here denied
The summer's sun, the spring's sweet dew,
That clothe with many a varied hue
The bleakest mountain-side.

Lord of the Isles, iii 14.

Strath Aird, finding that visitors injured it, by breaking and carrying away the stalactites with which it abounds, has secured this cavern by an eight or nine feet wall, with a door. Upon enquiring for the key, we found it was three miles up the loch at the laird's house. It was now late, and to stay until a messenger had gone and returned three miles was not to be thought of, any more than the alternative of going up the loch and lying there all night. We therefore, with regret, resolved to scale the wall, in which attempt, by the assistance of a rope and some ancient acquaintance with orchard breaking, we easily succeeded. The first entrance to this celebrated cave is rude and unpromising, but the light of the torches with which we were provided is soon reflected from roof, floor, and walls, which seem as if they were sheeted with marble, partly smooth, partly rough with frost-work and rustic ornaments, and partly wrought into statuary. The floor forms a steep and difficult ascent, and might be fancifully compared to a sheet of water, which, while it rushed whitening and foaming down a declivity, had been suddenly arrested and consolidated by the spell of an enchanter. Upon attaining the summit of this ascent, the cave descends with equal rapidity to the brink of a pool of the most limpid water, about four or five yards broad. There opens beyond this pool a portal arch, with beautiful white chasing upon the sides, which promises a continuation of the cave. One of our sailors swam across, for there was no other mode of passing, and informed us (as indeed we partly saw by the light he carried) that the enchantment of Macallister's cave terminated with this portal, beyond which there was only a rude ordinary cavern speedily choked with stones and earth. But the pool, on the brink of which we stood, surrounded by the most fanciful mouldings in a substance resembling white marble, and distinguished by the depth and purity of its waters, might be the bathing grotto of a Naiad. I think a statuary might catch beautiful hints from the fanciful and romantic disposition of the stalactites. There is scarce a form or group that an active fancy may not trace among the grotesque ornaments which have been gradually moulded in this cavern by the dropping of the calcareous water, and its hardening into petrifactions; many of these have been destroyed by the senseless rage of appropriation among recent tourists, and the grotto has lost (I am informed), through the smoke of torches, much of that vivid silver tint which was originally one of its chief distinctions. But enough of beauty remains to compensate for all that may be lost. As the easiest mode of return, I slid down the polished sheet of marble which forms the rising ascent, and thereby injured my pantaloons in a way which my jacket is ill calculated to conceal. Our wearables, after a month's hard service, begin to be frail, and there are daily demands for repairs. Our eatables also begin to assume a real nautical appearance — no soft bread — milk a rare commodity — and those gentlemen most in favour with John Peters, the steward, who prefer salt beef to fresh. To make amends, we never hear of sea-sickness, and the good-humour and harmony of the party continue uninterrupted. When we left the cave we carried off two grandsons of Mr. Macallister's, remarkably fine boys and Erskine, who may be called *L'ami des enfans*, treated them most kindly, and showed them all the curiosities in the vessel, causing even the guns to be fired for their amusement, besides filling their pockets with almonds and raisins. So that, with a handsome letter of apology, I hope we may erase any evil impression Mr. Macallister may adopt from our storming the exterior defences of his cavern. After having sent them ashore in safety, stand out of the bay with little or no wind, for the opposite island of Egg.

26th August, 1814. — At seven this morning were in the Sound which divides the Isle of Rum from that of Egg. Rum is rude, barren, and mountainous; Egg, although hilly and rocky, and traversed by one remarkable ridge called Scuir-Egg, has, in point of soil, a much more promising appearance. Southward of both lies Muick, or Muck, a low and fertile island, and though the least, yet probably the most valuable of the three. Caverns being still the order of the day, we man the boat and row along the shore of Egg, in quest of that which was the memorable scene of a horrid feudal vengeance. We had rounded more than half the island, admiring the entrance of many a bold natural cave which its rocks exhibit, but without finding that which we sought, until we procured a guide. This noted cave has a very narrow entrance, through which one can hardly creep on knees and hands. It rises steep and lofty within, and runs into the bowels of the rock to the depth of 255 measured feet. The height at the entrance may be about three feet, but rises to eighteen or twenty, and the breadth may vary in the same proportion. The rude and stony bottom of this cave is strewed with the bones of men, women, and children, being the sad relics of the ancient inhabitants of the island, 200 in number, who were slain on the following occasion:— The Macdonalds of the Isle of Egg, a people dependent on Clanranald, had done some injury to the Laird of Macleod. The tradition of the isle says that it was by a personal attack on the chieftain, in which his back was broken; but that of the other isles bears that the injury was offered to two or three of the Macleods, who, landing upon Egg and using some freedom with the young women, were seized by the islanders, bound hand and foot, and turned adrift in a boat, which the winds and waves safely conducted to Skye. To avenge the offence given; Macleod sailed with such a body of men as rendered resistance hopeless. The natives, fearing his vengeance, concealed themselves in this cavern, and after strict search, the Macleods went on board their galleys, after doing what mischief they could, concluding the inhabitants had left the isle. But next morning they espied from their vessel a man upon the island, and, immediately landing again, they traced his retreat, by means of a light snow on the ground, to this cavern. Macleod then summoned the subterraneous garrison, and demanded that the individuals who had offended him should be delivered up. This was peremptorily refused. The chieftain thereupon caused his people to divert the course of a rill of water, which falling over the mouth of the cave, would have prevented his purposed vengeance. He then kindled at the entrance of the cavern a huge fire, and maintained it until all within were destroyed by suffocation. The date of this dreadful deed must have been recent, if one can judge from the fresh appearance of those relics. I brought off, in spite of the prejudices of our sailors, a skull, which seems that of a young woman.

Before re-embarking, we visit another cave opening to the sea, but of a character widely different, being a large open vault as high as that of a cathedral, and running back a great way into the rock at the same height; the height and width of the opening give light to the whole. Here, after 1745, when the Catholic priests were scarcely tolerated, the priest of Egg used to perform the Romish service. A huge ledge of rock, almost half-way up one side of the vault, served for altar and pulpit; and the appearance of a priest and Highland congregation in such an extraordinary place of worship might have engaged the pencil of Salvator. Most of the inhabitants of Egg are still

Catholics, and laugh at their neighbours of Rum, who, having been converted by the cane of their chieftain, are called *Protestants of the yellow stick*. The Presbyterian minister and Catholic priest live upon this little island on very good terms. The people here were much irritated against the men of a revenue vessel who had seized all the stills, etc., in the neighbouring Isle of Muck, with so much severity as to take even the people's bedding. We had been mistaken for some time for this obnoxious vessel. Got on board about two o'clock, and agreed to stand over for Coll, and to be ruled by the wind as to what was next to be done. Bring up my journal.

27th August, 1814. — The wind, to which we resigned. ourselves, proves exceedingly tyrannical, and blows squally the whole night, which, with the swell of the Atlantic, now unbroken by any islands to windward, proves a means of great combustion in the cabin. The dishes and glasses in the steward's cupboards become locomotive-portmanteaus and writing-desks are more active than necessary — it is scarce possible to keep one's self within bed, and impossible to stand upright if you rise. Having crept upon deck about four in the morning, I find we are beating to windward off the Isle of Tyree, with the determination on the part of Mr. Stevenson that his constituents should visit a reef of rocks called *Skerry Vhor*, where he thought it would be essential to have a lighthouse. Loud remonstrances on the part of the Commissioners, who one and all declare they will subscribe to his opinion, whatever it may be, rather than continue this infernal buffeting. Quiet perseverance on the part of Mr. S., and great kicking, bouncing, and squabbling upon that of the Yacht, who seems to like the idea of Skerry Vhor as little as the Commissioners. At length, by dint of exertion, come in sight of this long ridge of rocks (chiefly under water), on which the tide breaks in a most tremendous style. There appear a few low broad rocks at one end of the reef, which is about a mile in length. These are never entirely under water, though the surf dashes over them. To go through all the forms, Hamilton, Duff, and I resolve to land upon these bare rocks in company with Mr. Stevenson. Pull through a very heavy swell with great difficulty, and approach a tremendous surf dashing over black pointed rocks. Our rowers, however, get the boat into a quiet creek between two rocks, where we contrive to land well wetted. I saw nothing remarkable in my way, excepting several seals, which we might have shot, but, in the doubtful circumstances of the landing, we did not care to bring guns. We took possession of the rock in name of the Commissioners, and generously bestowed our own great names on its crags and creeks. The rock was carefully measured by Mr. S. It will be a most desolate position for a lighthouse — the Bell Rock and Eddystone a joke to it, for the nearest land is the wild island of Tyree, at fourteen miles' distance. So much for the Skerry Vhor.

Came on board proud of our achievement; and, to the great delight of all parties, put the ship before the wind, and run swimmingly down for Iona. See a large square-rigged vessel, supposed an American. Reach Iona about five o'clock. The inhabitants of the isle of Columba, understanding their interest as well as as if they had been Deal boatmen, charged two guineas for Pilotage which Captain W. abridged into fifteen shillings too much for ten minutes' work. We soon got on shore, and landed in the bay of Martyrs, beautiful for its white sandy beach. Here all dead bodies are still landed, and laid for a time upon a small rocky eminence, called the Sweyne, before they are interred. Iona, the last time I saw it, seemed to me to contain the most wretched people I had anywhere seen. But either they have got better since I was here, or my eyes, familiarized with wretchedness of Zetland and the Harris, are less shocked with that of Iona. Certainly their houses are better thaneither, and the appearance of the people not worse. This little fertile isle contains upwards of 400 inhabitants, all living upon small farms, which they divide and subdivide as their families increase, so that the country is greatly over-peopled, and in some danger of a famine in case of a year of scarcity. Visit the nunnery and Reilig Oran, or burial-place of St. Oran, but the night coming on we return on board.

28th August, 1814. — Carry our breakfast ashore — take that repast in the house of Mr. Maclean, the schoolmaster and cicerone of the island — and resume our investigation of the ruins of the cathedral and the cemetery. Of these monuments, more than of any other, it may be said with propriety,

> You never tread upon them but you set
> Your feet upon some ancient history.

I do not mean to attempt a description of what is so well known as the ruins of Iona. Yet I think it has been as yet inadequately performed, for the vast number of carved tombs containing the reliques of the great, exceeds credibility. In general, even in the most noble churches, the number of the vulgar dead exceed in all proportion the few of eminence who are deposited under monuments. Iona is in all respects the reverse; until lately the inhabitants of the isle did not presume to mix their vulgar dust with that of chiefs, reguli, and abbots. The number, therefore, of carved and inscribed tombstones is quite marvellous, and I can easily credit the story told by Sacheverell, who assures us that 300 inscriptions had been collected, and were lost in the troubles of the 17th century. Even now, many more might be deciphered than have yet been made public, but the rustic step of the peasants and of Sassenach visitants is fast destroying these faint memorials of the valiant of the isles. A skilful antiquary remaining here a week, and having (or assuming) the power of raising the half-sunk monuments, might make a curious collection. We could only gaze and grieve; yet had the day not been Sunday, we would have brought our seamen ashore, and endeavoured to have raised some of these monuments. The celebrated ridges called *Jomaire na'n Righrean*, or Graves of the Kings, can now scarce be said to exist, though their site is still pointed out. Undoubtedly, the thirst of spoil, and the frequent custom of burying treasures with the ancient princes, occasioned their early violation; nor am I any sturdy believer in their being regularly ticketed off by inscriptions into the tombs of the Kings of Scotland, of Ireland, of Norway, and so forth. If such inscriptions ever existed, I should deem them the work of some crafty bishop or abbot, for the credit of his diocese or convent. Macbeth is said to have been the last King of Scotland here buried; sixty preceded him, all doubtless as powerful in their day, but now unknown — *carent quia vate sacro*. A few weeks' labour of Shakspeare, an obscure player, has done more for the memory of Macbeth than all the gifts, wealth, and monuments of this cemetery of princes have been able to secure to the rest of its inhabitants. It also occurred to me in Iona (as it has on many similar occasions) that the traditional recollections concerning the monks themselves are wonderfully faint, contrasted with the beautiful and interesting monuments of architecture which they have left behind them. In Scotland particularly, the people have frequently traditions wonderfully vivid of the persons and achievements of ancient warriors, whose towers have long been levelled with the soil. But of the monks of Melrose, Kelso, Aberbrothock, Iona, etc. etc. etc., they can tell nothing but that such a race existed, and inhabited the stately ruins of these monasteries. The quiet, slow, and uniform life of those recluse beings glided on, it may be, like a dark and silent stream, fed from unknown resources, and vanishing from the eye without leaving any marked trace of its course. The life of the chieftain was a mountain torrent thundering over rock and precipice, which, less deep and profound in itself, leaves on the minds of the terrified spectators those deep impressions of awe and wonder which are most readily handed down to posterity.

Among the various monuments exhibited at Iona is one where a Maclean lies in the same grave with one of the Macfies or Macduffies of Colonsay, with whom he had lived in alternate friendship and enmity during their lives. "He lies above him during death," said one if Maclean's followers, as his chief was interred, "as he was above him during life." There is a very ancient monument lying among those of the Macleans, but perhaps more ancient than any of them; it has a knight riding on horseback, and behind him a minstrel playing on a harp; this is conjectured to be Reginald Macdonald of the Isles, but there seems no reason for disjoining him from his kindred who sleep in the cathedral. A supposed ancestor of the Stewarts called Paul Purser, or Paul the Purse-bearer (treasurer to the King of Scotland), is said to lie under a stone near the Lord of the Isles. Most of the monuments engraved by Pennant are still in the same state of preservation, as are the few ancient crosses which are left. What a sight Iona must have been, when 360 crosses, of the same size and beautiful workmanship, were ranked upon the little rocky ridge of eminences which form the background to the cathedral! Part of the tower of the cathedral has fallen since I was here. It would require a better architect than I am, to say anything concerning the antiquity of these ruins, but I conceive those of the nunnery and of the *Reilig nan Oran*, or Oran's chapel, are decidedly the most ancient. Upon the cathedral and buildings attached to it there are marks of repairs at different times, some of them a late date, being obviously designed not to enlarge the buildings but to retrench them. We take a reluctant leave of Iona, and go on board.

The haze and dulness of the atmosphere seem to render it dubious if we can proceed, as we intended, to Staffa to-day — for mist among these islands is rather unpleasant. Erskine reads prayers on deck to all hands, and introduces a very apt allusion to our being now in sight of the first Christian Church from which Revelation was diffused over Scotland and all its islands. There is a very good form of prayer for the Lighthouse Service, composed by the Rev. Mr. Brunton.[1] A pleasure vessel lies under our lee from Belfast, with an Irish party related to Macneil of Colonsay. The haze is fast degenerating into downright rain, and that right heavy-verifying the words of Collins—

> And thither where beneath the showery west
> The mighty Kings of three fair realms are laid.[2]

After dinner, the weather being somewhat cleared, sailed for Staffa, and took boat. The surf running heavy up between the island and the adjacent rock, called Booshala, we landed at a creek near the Cormorant's cave. The mist now returned so thick as to hide all view of Iona, which was our landmark; and although Duff, Stevenson, and I had been formerly on the isle, we could not agree upon the proper road to the cave. I engaged myself, with Duff and Erskine, in a clamber of great toil and danger, and which at length brought me to the *Cannonball*, as they call a round granite stone moved by the sea up and down in a groove of rock, which it has worn for itself, with a noise resembling thunder. Here I gave up my research, and returned to my companions, who had not been more fortunate. As night was now falling, we resolved to go aboard and postpone the adventure of the enchanted cavern until next day. The yacht came to an anchor with the purpose of remaining off the island all night, but the hardness of the ground, and the weather becoming squally, obliged us to return to our safer mooring at Y-Columb-Kill.

29th August, 1814. — Night squally and rainy — morning ditto — we weigh, however, and return toward Staffa, and, very happily, the

---

[1] The Rev. Alexander Brunton, D.D., now (1836) Professor of Oriental Languages in the University of Edinburgh.

[2] Ode on the Superstitions of the Highlands.

View from the Isle of Staffa

day clears as we approach the isle. As we ascertained the situation of the cave, I shall only make this memorandum, that when the weather will serve, the best landing is to the lee of Booshala, a little conical islet or rock, composed of basaltic columns placed in an oblique or sloping position. In this way, you land at once on the flat causeway, formed by the heads of truncated pillars, which leads to the cave. But if the state of tide renders it impossible to land under Booshala, then take one of the adjacent creeks; in which case, keeping to the left hand along the top of the ledge of rocks which girdles in the isle, you find a dangerous and precipitous descent to the causeway aforesaid, from the table. Here we were under the necessity of towing our Commodore, Hamilton, whose gallant heart never fails him, whatever the tenderness of his toes may do. He was successfully lowered by a rope down the precipice, and proceeding along the flat terrace or causeway already mentioned, we reached the celebrated cave. I am not sure whether I was not more affected by this second, than by the first view of it. The stupendous columnar side walls — the depth and strength of the ocean with which the cavern is filled — the variety of tints formed by stalactites dropping and petrifying between the pillars, and resembling a sort of chasing of yellow or cream-coloured marble filling the interstices of roof — the corresponding variety below, where the ocean rolls over a red, and in some places a violet-coloured rock, the basis of the basaltic pillars — the dreadful noise of those august billows so well corresponding with the grandeur of the scene — are all circumstances elsewhere unparalleled. We have now seen in our voyage the three grandest caverns in Scotland, Smowe, Macallister's cave, and Staffa; so that, like the Troglodytes of yore, we may be supposed to know something of the matter. It is, however, impossible to compare scenes of natures so different, nor, were I compelled to assign a preference to any of the three, could I do it but with reference to their distinct characters, which might affect different individuals in different degrees. The characteristic of the Smowe cave may in this case be called the terrific, for the difficulties which oppose the stranger are of a nature so uncommonly wild as, for the first time at least, convey an impression of terror — with which the scenes to which he is introduced fully correspond. On the other hand, the dazzling whiteness of the incrustations in Macallister's cave, the elegance of the entablature, the beauty of its limpid pool, and the graceful dignity of its arch, render its leading features those of severe and chastened beauty. Staffa, the third of these subterraneous wonders, may challenge sublimity as it's principal characteristic. Without the savage gloom of the Smowe cave, and investigated with more apparent ease, though, perhaps, with equal real danger, the stately regularity of its columns forms a contrast to the grotesque imagery of Macallister's cave, combining at once the sentiments of grandeur and beauty. The former is, however, predominant, as it must necessarily be in any scene of the kind.

We had scarce left Staffa when the wind and rain returned. It was Erskine's object and mine to dine at Torloisk on Loch Tua, the seat of my valued friend Mrs. Maclean Clephane, and her accomplished daughters. But in going up Loch Tua between Ulva and Mull with this purpose,

> So thick was the mist on the ocean green,
> Nor cape nor headland could be seen.[1]

It was late before we came to anchor in a small bay presented by the little island of Gometra, which may be regarded as a continuation of Ulva. We therefore dine aboard, and after dinner, Erskine and I take the boat and row across the loch under a heavy rain. We could not see the house of Torloisk, so very thick was the haze, and we were a good deal puzzled how and where to achieve a landing; at length, espying a cart-road, we resolved to trust to its guidance, as we knew we must be near the house. We therefore went ashore with our servants, à la bonne aventure, under a drizzling rain. This was soon a matter of little consequence, for the necessity of crossing a swollen brook wetted me considerably, and Erskine, whose foot slipped, most completely. In wet and weary plight we reached the house, after a walk of a mile, in darkness, dirt, and rain, and it is hardly necessary to say that the pleasure of seeing our friends soon banished all recollection of our unpleasant voyage and journey.

30th August, 1814. — The rest of our friends come ashore by invitation, and breakfast with the ladies, whose kindness would fain have delayed us for a few days, and at last condescended to ask for one day only — but even this could not be, our time wearing short.

1   So thick a haze o'erspreads the sky,
    They cannot see the Sun on high.

> Southey's *Inchcape Rock*.

Torloisk is finely situated upon the coast of Mull, facing Staffa. It is a good comfortable house, to which Mrs. Clephane has made some additions. The grounds around have been dressed, so as to smooth their ruggedness, without destroying the irregular and wild character peculiar to the scene and country. In this, much taste has been displayed. At Torloisk, as at Dunvegan, trees grow freely and rapidly, and the extensive plantations formed by Mrs. C. serve to show that nothing but a little expense and patience on the part of the proprietors, with attention to planting in proper places at first, and in keeping up fences afterwards, are awanting to remove the reproach of nakedness, so often thrown upon the Western Isles. With planting comes shelter, and the proper allotment and division of fields. With all this Mrs. Clephane is busied, and, I trust, successfully; I am sure, actively and usefully. Take leave of my fair friends, with regret that I cannot prolong my stay for a day or two. When we come on board, we learn that Staffa-Macdonald is just come to his house of Ulva; this is a sort of unpleasant dilemma, for we cannot now go there without some neglect towards Mrs. Maclean Clephane; and, on the other hand, from his habits with all of us, he may be justly displeased with our quitting his very threshold without asking for him. However, upon the whole matter, and being already under weigh, we judged it best to work out of the loch, and continue our purpose of rounding the northern extremity of Mull, and then running down the Sound between Mull and the mainland. We had not long pursued our voyage before we found it was like to be a very slow one. The wind fell away entirely, and after repeated tacks we could hardly clear the extreme north-western point of Mull by six o'clock — which must have afforded amusement to the ladies whose hospitable entreaties we had resisted, as we were almost all the while visible from Torloisk. A fine evening, but scarce a breath of wind.

31st August, 1814. —Went on deck between three and four in the morning, and found the vessel almost motionless in a calm sea, scarce three miles advanced on her voyage. We had, however, rounded the north western side of Mull, and were advancing between the north eastern side and the rocky and wild shores of Ardnamurchan on the mainland of Scotland. Astern were visible in bright moonlight the distant mountains of Rum; yet nearer, the remarkable ridge in the isle of Egg, called Scuir-Egg; and nearest of all the low isle of Muick. After enjoying this prospect for some time, returned to my berth. Rise before eight — a delightful day, but very calm, and the little wind there is decidedly against us. Creeping on slowly, we observe, upon the shore of Ardnamurchan, a large old castle — called Mingary. It appears to be surrounded with a very high wall, forming a kind of polygon, in order to adapt itself to the angles of a precipice overhanging the sea, on which the castle is founded. Within or beyond the wall, and probably forming part of an inner court, I observed a steep roof and windows, probably of the 17th century. The whole, as seen with a spy-glass, seems ruinous. As we proceed, we open on the left hand Loch Sunart, running deep into the mainland, crossed by distant ridges of rocks, and terminating apparently among the high mountains above Strontian. On the right hand we open the Sound of Mull, and pass the Bloody Bay, which acquired that name from a desperate battle fought between an ancient Lord of the Isles and his son. The latter was assisted by the Macleans of Mull, then in the plenitude of their power, but was defeated. This was a sea-fight; galleys being employed on each side. It has bequeathed a name to a famous pibroch.

Proceeding southward, we open the beautiful bay of Tobermory, or Mary's Well. The mouth of this fine natural roadstead is closed by an isle called Colvay, having two passages, of which only one, the northerly, is passable for ships. The bay is surrounded by steep hills, covered with copsewood, through which several brooks seek the sea in a succession of beautiful cascades. The village has been established as a fishing station by the Society for British Fisheries. The houses along the quay are two and three stories high, and well built; the feuars paying to the Society sixpence per foot of their line of front. On the top of a steep bank, rising above the first town, runs another line of second-rate cottages, which pay fourpence per foot; and behind are huts, much superior to the ordinary sheds of the country, which pay only twopence per foot. The town is all built upon a regular plan, laid down by the Society. The new part is reasonably clean, and the old not unreasonably dirty. We landed at an excellent quay, which is not yet finished, and found the little place looked thriving and active. The people were getting in their patches of corn; and the shrill voices of the children, attending their parents in the field, and loading the little ponies which are used in transporting the grain, formed a chorus not disagreeable to those whom it reminds of similar sounds at home. The praise of comparative cleanliness does not extend to the lanes around Tobermory, in one of which I had nearly been effectually bogged. But the richness of the round steep green knolls, clothed with copse, and glancing with cascades, and a pleasant peep at a small fresh-water loch embosomed among them — the view of the bay, surrounded and guarded by the island of Colvay — the gliding of two or three vessels in the more distant Sound — and the row of the gigantic Ardnamurchan mountains closing the scene to the north, almost justify the eulogium of Sacheverell, who, in 1688, declared the bay of Tobermory might equal any prospect in Italy. It is said that Sacheverell made some money by weighing up the treasures lost in the Florida, a vessel of the Spanish Armada, which was wrecked in the harbour. He himself affirms, that though the use of the diving-bells was at first successful, yet the attempt was afterwards disconcerted by bad weather.

Tobermory takes its name from a spring dedicated to the Virgin, which was graced by a chapel; but no vestiges remain of the chapel, and the spring rises in the middle of a swamp, whose depth and dirt discouraged the nearer approach of Protestant pilgrims. Mr. Stevenson, whose judgment is unquestionable, thinks that the village should have been built on the island called Colvay, and united to the continent by a key, or causeway, built along the southernmost channel, which is very shallow. By this means the people would have been much nearer the fishings, than retired into the depth of the bay.

About three o'clock we get on board, and a brisk and favourable breeze arises, which carries us smoothly down the Sound. We soon pass Arros, with its fragment of a castle, behind which is the house of Mr. Maxwell (an odd name for this country), chamberlain to the Duke of Argyle, which reminds me of much kindness and hospitality received from him and Mr. Stewart, the sheriff-substitute, when I was formerly in Mull. On the shore of Morven, on the opposite side, pass the ruins of a small fortalice, called Donagail, situated as usual on a precipice overhanging the sea. The "woody Morven," though the quantity of shaggy diminutive copse, which springs up where it obtains any shelter, still shows that it must once have merited the epithet, is now, as visible from the Sound of Mull, a bare country — of which the hills towards the sea have a slope much resembling those in Selkirkshire, and accordingly afford excellent pasture, and around several farm-houses well cultivated and improved fields. I think I observe considerable improvement in husbandry, even since I was here last; but there is a difference in coming from Oban and Cape Wrath. — Open Loch Alline, a beautiful salt-water lake, with a narrow outlet to the Sound. It is surrounded by round hills, sweetly fringed with green copse below, and one of which exhibits to the spy-glass ruins of a castle. There is great promise of beauty in its interior, but we cannot see everything. The land on the southern bank of the entrance slopes away into a sort of promontory, at the extremity of which are the very imperfect ruins of the castle of Ardtornish, to which the Lords of the Isles summoned parliaments, and from whence one of them dated a treaty with the Crown of England as an independent Prince. These ruins are seen to most advantage from the south, where they are brought into a line with one high fragment towards the west predominating over the rest. The shore of the promontory on the south side becomes rocky, and when it slopes round to the west, rises into a very bold and high precipitous bank, skirting the bay on the western side, partly cliffy, partly covered with brushwood, with various streams dashing over it from a great height. Above the old castle of Ardtornish, and about where the promontory joins the land, stands the present mansion, a neat white-washed house, with several well-enclosed and well-cultivated fields surrounding it.

The high and dignified character assumed by the shores of Morven after leaving Ardtornish continues till we open the Loch Linnhe, the commencement of the great chain of inland lakes running up to Fort-William, and which it is proposed to unite with Inverness by means of the Caledonian Canal. The wisdom of the plan adopted in this national measure seems very dubious. Had the Canal been of more moderate depth, and the burdens imposed upon passing vessels less expensive, there can be no doubt that the coasters, sloops, and barks would have carried on a good trade by means of it. But the expense and plague of locks, etc., may prevent these humble vessels from taking this abridged voyage, while ships above twenty or thirty tons will hesitate to engage themselves in the intricacies of a long lake navigation, exposed, without room for manoeuvring, to all the sudden squalls of the mountainous country. Ahead of us, in the mouth of Loch Linnhe, lies the low and fertile isle of Lismore, formerly the appanage of the Bishops of the Isles, who, as usual, knew where to choose church patrimony. The coast of the Mull, on the right hand of the Sound, has a black, rugged, and unimproved character. Above Scallister Bay are symptoms of improvement. Moonlight has risen upon us as we pass Duart Castle, now an indistinct mass upon its projecting promontory. It was garrisoned for Government so late as 1780, but is now ruinous. We see, at about a mile's distance, the fatal shelve on which Duart exposed the daughter of Argyle, on which Miss Baillie's play of the Family Legend is founded, but now,

> Without either sign or sound of their shock,
> The waves flowed over the Lady's rock.[1]

The placid state of the sea is very different from what I have seen it, when six stout rowers could scarce give a boat headway through the conflicting tides. These fits of violence so much surprised and offended a body of the Camerons, who were bound upon some expedition to Mull, and had been accustomed to the quietness of lake navigation, that they drew their dirks, and began to stab the waves — from which popular tale this run of tide is called *the Men of Lochaber*. The weather being delightfully moderate, we agree to hover hereabout all night, or anchor under the Mull shore, should it be necessary, in order to see Dunstaffnage tomorrow morning. The isle of Kerrera is now in sight, forming the bay of Oban. Beyond lie the varied and magnificent summits of the chain of mountains bordering Loch Linnhe, as well as those between Loch Awe and Loch Etive, over which the summit of Ben Cruachan is proudly prominent. Walk on deck, admiring this romantic propect until ten; then below, and turn in.

1st September, 1814. — Rise betwixt six and seven, and having discreetly secured our breakfast, take boat for the old castle of Dunstaffnage, situated upon a promontory on the side of Loch Linnhe and near to Loch Etive. Nothing could exceed the beauty of the day and of the prospect. We coasted the low, large, and fertile isle of Lismore, where a Catholic Bishop, Chisholm, has established a seminary of young men intended for priests, and what is a better thing,

---

[1]   Southey's *Inchcape Rock*.

Dunstaffnage

a valuable lime-work. Report speaks well of the lime, but indifferently of the progress of the students. Tacking to the shore of the loch, we land at Dunstaffnage, once, it is said, the seat of the Scottish monarchy, till success over the Picts and Saxons transferred their throne to Scoone, Dunfermline, and at length to Edinburgh. The castle is still the King's (nominally), and the Duke of Argyle (nominally also) is hereditary keeper. But the real right of property is in the family of the depute-keeper, to which it was assigned as an appanage, the first possessor being a natural son of an Earl of Argyle. The shell of the castle, for little more now remains, bears marks of extreme antiquity. It is square in form, with round towers at three of the angles, and is situated upon a lofty precipice, carefully scarped on all sides to render it perpendicular. The entrance is by a staircase, which conducts you to a wooden landing-place in front of the portal-door. This landing-place could formerly be raised at pleasure, being of the nature of a draw-bridge. When raised, the place was inaccessible. You pass under an ancient arch, with a low vault (being the porter's lodge) on the right hand, and flanked by loop-holes, for firing upon any hostile guest who might force his passage thus far. This admits you into the inner court, which is about eighty feet square. It contains two mean-looking buildings, about sixty or seventy years old; the ancient castle having been consumed by fire in 1715. It is said that the nephew of the proprietor was the incendiary. We went into the apartments, and found they did not exceed the promise of the exterior; but they admitted us to walk upon the battlements of the old castle, which displayed a most splendid prospect. Beneath, and far projected into the loch, were seen the woods and houses of Campbell of Lochnell. A little summer-house, upon an eminence, belonging to this wooded bank, resembles an ancient monument. On the right, Loch Etive, after pouring its waters like a furious cataract over a strait called Connell Ferry, comes between the castle and a round island belonging to its demesne, and nearly insulates the situation. In front is a low rocky eminence on the opposite side of the arm, through which Loch Etive flows into Loch Linnhe. Here was situated *Beregenium*, once, it is said, a British capital city; and, as our informant told us, the largest market-town in Scotland. Of this splendour are no remains but a few trenches and excavations, which the distance did not allow us to examine. The ancient masonry of Dunstaffnage is mouldering fast under time and neglect. The foundations are beginning to decay, and exhibit gaps between the rock and the wall; and the battlements are become ruinous. The inner court is encumbered with ruins. A hundred pounds or two would put this very ancient fortress in a state of preservation for ages, but I fear this is not to be expected. The stumps of large trees, which had once shaded the vicinity of the castle, gave symptoms of decay in the family of Dunstaffnage. We were told of some ancient spurs and other curiosities preserved in the castle, but they were locked up. In the vicinity of the castle is a chapel which had once been elegant, but by the building up of windows, etc., is now heavy enough. I have often observed that the means adopted in Scotland for repairing old buildings are generally as destructive of their grace and beauty, as if that had been the express object. Unfortunately, most churches, particularly, have gone through both stages of destruction, having been first repaired by the building up of the beautiful shafted windows, and then the roof being suffered to fall in, they became ruins indeed, but without any touch of the picturesque farther than their massive walls and columns may afford. Near the chapel of Dunstaffnage is a remarkable echo.

Re-embarked, and, rowing about a mile and a half or better along the shore of the lake, again landed under the ruins of the old castle of Dunolly. This fortress, which, like that of Dunstaffnage, forms a marked feature in this exquisite landscape, is situated on a bold and precipitous promontory overhanging the lake. The principal part of the ruins now remaining is a square tower or keep of the ordinary size, which had been the citadel of the castle; but fragments of other buildings, overgrown with ivy, show that Dunolly had once been a place of considerable importance. These had enclosed a court-yard, of which the keep probably formed one side, the entrance being by a very steep ascent from the land side, which had formerly been cut across by a deep moat, and defended doubtless by outworks and a drawbridge. Beneath the castle stands the modern house of Dunolly, a decent mansion, suited to the reduced state of the MacDougalls of Lorn, who, from being Barons powerful enough to give battle to and defeat Robert Bruce, are now declined into private gentlemen of moderate fortune.

This very ancient family is descended from Somerled, Thane, or rather, under that name, *King* of Argyle and the Hebrides. He had two sons, to one of whom he left his insular possessions — and he became founder of the dynasty of the Lords of the Isles, who maintained a stirring independence during the Middle Ages. The other was founder of the family of the MacDougalls of Lorn. One of them being married to a niece of the Red Cumming, in revenge of his slaughter at Dumfries, took a vigorous part against Robert Bruce in his struggles to maintain the independence of Scotland. At length the King, turning his whole strength towards MacDougall, encountered him at a pass near Loch Awe; but the Highlanders, being possessed of the strong ground, compelled Bruce to retreat, and again gave him battle at Dalry, near Tynedrum, where he had concentrated his forces. Here he was again defeated, and the tradition of the MacDougall family bears that in the conflict the Lord of Lorn engaged hand to hand with Bruce, and was struck down by that monarch. As they grappled together on the ground, Bruce being uppermost, a vassal of MacDougall, called MacKeoch, relieved his master by pulling Bruce from him. In this close struggle the King left his mantle and brooch in the hands of his enemies, and the latter trophy was long preserved in the family, until it was lost in an accidental fire. Barbour tells the same story, but I think with circumstances somewhat different. When Bruce had gained the throne for which he fought so long, he displayed his resentment against the MacDougalls of Lorn by depriving them of the greatest part of their domains, which were bestowed chiefly upon the Steward of Scotland. Sir Colin Campbell, the Knight of Loch Awe, and the Knight of Glenurchy, Sir Dugald Campbell, married daughters of the Steward, and received with them great portion of the forfeiture of MacDougall. Bruce even compelled or persuaded the Lord of the Isles to divorce his wife, who was a daughter of MacDougall, and take in marriage a relation of his own. The son of the divorced lady was not permitted to succeed to the principality of the Isles, on account of his connexion with the obnoxious MacDougall. But a large appanage was allowed him upon the Mainland, where he founded the family of Glengarry.

The family of MacDougall suffered farther reduction during the great civil war, in which they adhered to the Stewarts, and in 1715 they forfeited the small estate of Dunolly, which was then all that remained of what had once been a principality. The then representative of the family fled to France, and his son (father of the present proprietor) would have been without any means of education, but for the spirit of clanship, which induced one of the name, in the humble situation of keeper of a public house at Dumbarton, to take his young chief to reside with him, and be at the expense of his education and maintenance until his fifteenth or sixteenth year. He proved a clever and intelligent man, and made good use of the education he received. When the affair of 1745 was in agitation, it was expected by the south-western clans that Charles Edward would have landed near Oban, instead of which he disembarked at Loch-nan-augh, in Arisaig. Stuart of Appin sent information of his landing to MacDougall, who gave orders to his brother to hold the clan in readiness to rise, and went himself to consult with the chamberlain of the Earl of Breadalbane, who was also in the secret. He found this person indisposed to rise, alleging that Charles had disappointed them both in the place of landing, and the support he had promised. MacDougall then resolved to play cautious, and went to visit the Duke of Argyle, then residing at Roseneath, probably without any determined purpose as to his future proceedings. While he was waiting the Duke's leisure, he saw a horseman arrive at full gallop, and shortly after, the Duke entering the apartment where MacDougall was, with a map in his hand, requested him, after friendly salutations, to point out Loch-nan-augh on that map. MacDougall instantly saw that the secret of Charles's landing had transpired, and resolved to make a merit of being the first who should give details. The persuasions of the Duke determined him to remain quiet, and the reward was the restoration of the little state of Dunolly, lost by his father in 1715. This gentleman lived to a very advanced stage of life, and was succeeded by Peter MacDougall, Esq., now of Dunolly. I had these particulars respecting the restoration of the estate from a near relation of the family, whom we met at Dunstaffnage.

The modern house of Dunolly is on the neck of land under the old castle, having on the one hand the lake with its islands and mountains; on the other, two romantic eminences tufted with copsewood, of which the higher is called Barmore, and is now planted. I have seldom seen a more romantic and delightful situation, to which the peculiar state of the family gave a sort of moral interest. Mrs.

MacDougall, observing strangers surveying the ruins, met us on our return, and most politely insisted upon our accepting fruit and refreshments. This was a compliment meant to absolute strangers, but when our names became known to her, the good lady's entreaties that we would stay till Mr. MacDougall returned from his ride, became very pressing. She was in deep mourning for the loss of an eldest son, who had fallen bravely in Spain and under Wellington, a death well becoming the descendant of so famed arace. The second son, a lieutenant in the navy, had, upon this family misfortune, obtained leave to visit his parents for the first time after many years' service, but had now returned to his ship. Mrs. M. spoke with melancholy pride of the death of her eldest son, with hope and animation of the prospects of the survivor. A third is educated for the law. Declining the hospitality offered us, Mrs. M. had the goodness to walk with us along the shore towards Oban, as far as the property of Dunolly extends, and showed us a fine spring, called *Tobar nan Gall*, or the Well of the Stranger, where our sailors supplied themselves with excellent water, which has been rather a scarce article with us, as it soon becomes past a landsman's use on board ship. On the seashore, about a quarter of a mile from the castle, is a huge fragment of the rock called *plum-pudding stone*, which art or nature has formed into a gigantic pillar. Here it is said Fion or Fingal tied his dog Bran — here also the celebrated Lord of the Isles tied up his dogs when he came upon a visit to the Lords of Lorn. Hence it is called *Clach nan Con; ie.* the Dog's Stone. A tree grew once on the top of this bare mass of composite stone, but it was cut down by a curious damsel of the family, who was desirous to see a treasure said to be deposited beneath it. Enjoyed a pleasant walk of a mile along the beach to Oban, a town of some consequence, built in a semicircular form, around a good harbour formed by the opposite isle of Kerrara, on which Mrs. M. pointed out the place where Alexander II. died, while, at the head of a powerful armament, he meditated the reduction of the Hebrides. The field is still called Dal-ry — the King's field.

Having taken leave of Mrs. MacDougall, we soon satisfied our curiosity concerning Oban, which owed its principal trade to the industry of two brothers, Messrs. Stevenson, who dealt in shipbuilding. One is now dead, the other almost retired from business, and trade is dull in the place. Heard of an active and industrious man, who had set up a nursery of young trees, which ought to succeed, since at present, whoever wants plants must send to Glasgow and how much the plants suffer during a voyage of such length, any one may conceive. Go on board after a day delightful for the serenity and clearness of the weather, as well as for the objects we had visited. I forgot to say, that through Mr. MacDougall's absence we lost an opportunity of seeing a bronze figure of one of his ancestors, called *Bacach*, or the lame, armed and mounted as for a tournament. The hero flourished in the twelfth century. After a grand council of war, we determine, as we are so near the coast of Ulster, that we will stand over and view the celebrated Giant's Causeway; and Captain Wilson receives directions accordingly.

2nd September, 1814. — Another most beautiful day. The heat, for the first time since we sailed from Leith, is somewhat incommodious; so we spread a handsome awning to save our complexions, God wot, and breakfast beneath it in style. The breeze is gentle, and quite favourable. It has conducted us from the extreme cape of Mull, called the Black Head of Mull, into the Sound of Islay. We view in passing that large and fertile island, the property of Campbell of Shawfield, who has introduced an admirable style of farming among his tenants. Still farther behind us retreats the island of Jura, with the remarkable mountains called the Paps of Jura, which form a landmark at a great distance. They are very high, but in our eyes, so much accustomed of late to immense height, do not excite much surprise. Still farther astern is the small isle of Scarba, which, as we see it, seems to be a single hill. In the passage or sound between Scarba and the extremity of Jura is a terrible run of tide, which, contending with the sunk rocks and islets of that foul channel, occasions the succession of whirlpools called the Gulf of Corrievreckan. Seen at this distance, we cannot judge of its terrors. The sight of Corrievreckan and of the low rocky isle of Colonsay, betwixt which and Islay we are now passing, strongly recalls to my mind poor John Leyden and his tale of the Mermaid and MacPhail of Colonsay.[1] Probably the name of the hero should have been MacFie, for to the MacDuffies (by abridgment MacFies) Colonsay

---

[1]   See Minstrelsy of the Border - Scott's Poetical Works, vol, iv. PP. 285-306.

of old pertained. It is said the last of these MacDuffies was executed as an oppressor by order of the Lord of the Isles, and lies buried in the adjacent small island of Oransay, where there is an old chapel with several curious monuments, which, to avoid losing this favourable breeze, we are compelled to leave unvisited. Colonsay now belongs to a gentleman named MacNeil. On the right beyond it opens at a distance the western coast of Mull, which we already visited in coming from the northward. We see the promontory of Ross, which is terminated by Y-Columb-Kill, also now visible. The shores of Loch Tua and Ulva are in the blue distance, with the little archipelago which lies around Staffa. Still farther, the hills of Rum can just be distinguished from the blue sky. We are now arrived at the extreme point of Islay, termed, from the strong tides, the *Runs of Islay*. We here only feel them as a large but soft swell of the sea, the weather being delightfully clear and serene. In the course of the evening we lose sight of the Hebrides, excepting Islay, having now attained the western side of that island.

3rd September, 1814. — In the morning early we are off Innistulhan, an islet very like Inchkeith in size and appearance, and like Inchkeith, displaying a lighthouse. Messrs. Hamilton, Duff, and Stevenson go ashore to visit the Irish lighthouse and compare notes. A fishing-boat comes off with four or five stout lads, without neckerchiefs or hats, and the best of whose joint garments selected would hardly equip an Edinburgh beggar. Buy from this specimen of Paddy in his native land some fine John Dories for threepence each. The mainland of Ireland adjoining to this island (being part of the county of Donegal) resembles Scotland, and though hilly, seems well cultivated upon the whole. A brisk breeze directly against us. We beat to windward by assistance of a strong tide-stream, in order to weather the head of Innishowen, which covers the entrance of Lough Foyle, with the purpose of running up the loch to see Londonderry, so celebrated for its siege in 1689.

But short tacks and long tacks were in vain, and at dinnertime, having lost our tide, we find ourselves at all disadvantage both against wind and sea. Much combustion at our meal, and the manoeuvres by which we attempted to eat and drink remind me of the enchanted drinking cup in the old ballad,—

Some shed it on their shoulder,
Some shed it on their thigh;
And he that did not hit his mouth
Was sure to hit his eye.

In the evening, backgammon and cards are in great request. We have had our guns shotted all this day for fear of the Yankees — a privateer having been seen off Tyree Islands, and taken some vessels — as is reported. — About nine o'clock weather the Innishowen head, and enter the Lough, and fire a gun as a signal for a pilot. The people here are great smugglers; and at the report of the gun we see several lights on shore disappear. — About the middle of the day too, our appearance (much resembling a revenue cutter) occasioned a smoke being made in the midst of a very rugged cliff on the shore — a signal probably to any of the smugglers' craft that might be at sea. Come to anchor in eight fathom water, expecting our pilot.

4th September, 1814. — Waked in the morning with good hope of hearing service in Derry Cathedral, as we had felt ourselves under weigh since daylight; but these expectations vanished when, going on deck, we found ourselves only half-way up Lough Foyle, and at least ten miles from Derry. Very little wind, and that against us and the navigation both shoally and intricate. Called a council of war; and after considering the difficulty of getting up to Derry, and the chance of being wind-bound when we do get there, we resolve to renounce our intended visit to that town. We had hardly put the ship about, when the Irish Æolus shifted his trumpet, and opposed our exit, as he had formerly been unfavourable to our progress up the lake. At length, we are compelled to betake ourselves to towing, the wind fading into an absolute calm. This gives us time enough to admire the northern, or Donegal, side of Lough Foyle — the other being hidden from us by haze and distance. Nothing can be more favourable than this specimen of Ireland. — A beautiful variety of cultivated slopes, intermixed with banks of wood; rocks skirted with a distant ridge of heathy hills, watered by various brooks; the glens or banks being in general, planted or covered with copse; and finally, studded by a succession of villas and gentlemen's seats, good farm-houses, and neat white-washed cabins. Some of the last are happily situated upon the verge of the sea, with banks of copse or a rock or two rising behind them, and the white sand in front. The land, in general, seems well cultivated and enclosed — but in some places the enclosures seem too small, and the ridges too crooked, for proper farming. We pass two gentlemen's seats, called White Castle and Red Castle; the last a large good-looking mansion, with trees, and a pretty vale sloping upwards from the sea. As we approach the termination of the Lough, the ground becomes more rocky and barren, and the cultivation interrupted by impracticable patches, which have been necessarily abandoned. Come in view of Green Castle, a large ruinous castle said to have belonged to the MacWilliams. The remains are romantically situated upon a green bank sloping down to the sea, and are partly covered with ivy. From their extent, the place must have been a chieftain's residence of the very first consequence. Part of the ruins appear to be founded upon a high red rock, which the eve at first blends with the masonry. To the east of the ruins, upon a cliff overhanging the sea, are a modern fortification and barrack-yard, and beneath, a large battery for protection of the shipping which may enter the Lough; the guns are not yet mounted. The Custom-house boat boards us and confirms the account that American cruisers are upon the coast. Drift out of the Lough, and leave behind us this fine country, all of which belongs in property to Lord Donegal; other possessors only having long leases, as sixty years, or so forth. Red Castle, however, before distinguished as a very good-looking house, is upon a perpetual lease. We discharge our pilot — the gentlemen go ashore with him in the boat, in order to put foot on Irish land. I shall defer that pleasure till I can promise myself something to see. When our gentlemen return, we read prayers on deck. After dinner go ashore at the small fishing-village of Port Rush, pleasantly situated upon a peninsula, which forms a little harbour. Here we are received by Dr. Richardson, the inventor of the fiorin-grass (or of some of its excellences). He cultivates this celebrated vegetable on a very small scale, his whole farm not exceeding four acres. Here I learn, with inexpressible surprise and distress, the death of one of the most valued of the few friends whom these memoranda might interest.[1] She was, indeed, a rare example of the soundest good sense, and the most exquisite purity of moral feeling, united with the utmost grace and elegance of personal beauty, and with manners becoming the most dignified rank in British society. There was a

[1]   Harriet, Duchess of Buccleuch, died Aug.24, 1814

feminine softness in all her deportment, which won universal love, as her firmness of mind and correctness of principle commanded veneration. To her family her loss is inexpressibly great. I know not whether it was the purity of her mind, or the ethereal cast of her features and form, but I could never associate in my mind her idea and that of mortality; so that the shock is the more heavy, as being totally unexpected. God grant comfort to the afflicted survivor and his family!

5th September, 1814. — Wake, or rather rise at six, for I have waked the whole night, or fallen into broken sleeps only to be hag-ridden by the nightmare. Go ashore with a heavy heart, to see sights which I had much rather leave alone. Land under Dunluce, a ruined castle built by the MacGilligans, or MacQuillens, but afterwards taken from them by a Macdonnell, ancestor of the Earls of Antrim, and destroyed by Sir John Perrot, Lord Lieutenant in the reign or Queen Elizabeth. This Macdonnell came from the Hebrides at the head of a Scottish colony. The site of the castle much resembles Dunnottar, but it is on a smaller scale. The ruins occupy perhaps more than an acre of ground, being the level top of a high rock advanced into the sea, by which it is surrounded on three sides, and divided from the mainland by a deep chasm. The access was by a narrow bridge, of which there now remains but a single rib, or ledge, forming a doubtful and a precarious access to the ruined castle. On the outer side of the bridge are large remains of outworks, probably for securing cattle, and for domestic offices — and the vestiges of a chapel. Beyond the bridge are an outer and inner gateway, with their defences. The large gateway forms one angle of the square enclosure of the fortress, and at the other landward angle is built a large round tower. There are vestiges of similar towers occupying the angles of the precipice overhanging the sea. These towers were connected by a curtain, on which artillery seems to have been mounted. Within this circuit are the ruins of an establishment of feudal grandeur on the large scale. The great hall, forming, it would seem, one side of the inner court, is sixty paces long lighted by windows which appear to have been shafted with stone, but are now ruined. Adjacent are the great kitchen and ovens, with a variety of other buildings, but no square tower, or keep. The most remarkable part of Dunluce, however, is, that the whole mass of plum-pudding rock on which the fort is built is completely perforated by a cave sloping downwards from the inside of the moat or dry-ditch beneath the bridge, and opening to the sea on the other side. It might serve the purpose of a small harbour, especially if they had, as is believed, a descent to the cave from within the castle. It is difficult to conceive the use of the aperture to the land, unless it was in some way enclosed and defended. Above the ruinous castle is a neat farm-house. Mrs. More, the good-wife, a Scoto-Hibernian, received us with kindness and hospitality which did honour to the nation of her birth, as well as of her origin, in a house whose cleanliness and neatness might have rivalled England. Her churn was put into immediate motion on our behalf, and we were loaded with all manner of courtesy, as well good things. We heard here of an armed schooner having been seen off the coast yesterday, which fired on a boat that went off to board her, and would seem therefore to be a privateer, or armed smuggler.

Return on board for breakfast, and then again take boat for the Giant's Causeway — having first shotted the guns, and agreed on a signal, in case this alarming stranger should again make his appearance. Visit two caves, both worth seeing, but not equal to those we have seen; one, called Port Coon, opens in a small cove, or bay — the outer reach opens into an inner cave, and that again into the sea. The other, called Down Kerry, is a sea-cave, like that on the eastern side of Loch Eribol — a high arch up which the sea rolls:— the weather being quiet we sailed in very nearly to the upper end. We then rowed on to the celebrated Causeway a platform composed of basaltic pillars, projecting into the sea like the pier of a harbour. As I was tired, and had a violent headache, I did not land, but could easily see that the regularity of the columns was the same as at Staffa; but that island contains a much more extensive and curious specimen of this curious phenomenon.

Row along the shores of this celebrated point, which are extremely striking as well as curious. They open into a succession of little bays, each of which has precipitous banks graced with long ranges of the basaltic pillars, sometimes placed above each other, and divided by masses of interweaving strata, or by green sloping banks of earth of extreme steepness. These remarkable ranges of columns are in some places chequered by horizontal strata of a red rock or earth, of the appearance of ochre; so that the green of the grassy banks, the dark-grey or black appearance of the columns, with those red seams and other varieties of the interposed strata, have most uncommon and striking effects. The outline of these cliffs is as singular as their colouring. In several places the earth has wasted away from single columns, and left them standing insulated and erect, like the ruined colonnade of an ancient temple, upon the verge of the precipice. In other places, the disposition of the basaltic ranges presents singular appearances, to which the guides give names agreeable to the images which they are supposed to represent. Each of the little bays or inlets has also its appropriate name. One is called the Spanish Bay, from one of the Spanish Armada having been wrecked there. Thus our voyage has repeatedly traced the memorable remnants of that celebrated squadron. The general name of the cape adjacent to the Causeway is Bengore Head. To those who have seen Staffa, the peculiar appearance of the Causeway itself will lose much of its effect; but the grandeur of the neighbouring scenery will still maintain the reputation of Bengore Head. The people ascribe all these wonders to Fin MacCoul, whom they couple with a Scottish giant called Ben-an something or other. The traveller is plied by guides, who make their profit by selling pieces of crystal, agate, or chalcedony, found in the interstices of the rocks. Our party brought off some curious joints of the columns, and, had I been quite as I am wont to be, I would have selected four to be capitals of a rustic porch at Abbotsford. But, alas! alas! I am much out of love with vanity at this moment. From what we hear at the Causeway we have every reason to think that the pretended privateer has been a gentleman's pleasure-vessel. — Continue our voyage southward, and pass between the Main of Ireland and the Isle of Rachrin, a rude heathy-looking island, once a place of refuge to Robert Bruce. This is said, in ancient times, to have been the abode of banditti, who plundered the neighbouring coast. At present it is under a long lease to a Mr. Gage, who is said to maintain excellent order among the islanders. Those of bad character he expels to Ireland, and hence it is a phrase among the people of Rachrin, when they wish ill to any one, "*May Ireland be his hinder end.*" On the Main we see the village of Ballintry, and a number of people collected, the remains of an Irish fair. Close by is a small island, called Sheep Island. We now take leave of the Irish coast, having heard nothing of its popular complaints, excepting that the good lady at Dunluce made a heavy moan against the tithes, which had compelled her husband to throw his whole farm into pasture. Stand over toward Scotland, and see the Mull of Cantyre light.

6th September, 1814. — Under the lighthouse at the Mull of Cantyre; situated on a desolate spot among rocks, like a Chinese pagoda in Indian drawings. Duff and Stevenson go ashore at six. Hamilton follows, but is unable to land, the sea having got up. The boat brings back letters, and I have the great comfort to learn all are well at Abbotsford. About eight the tide begins to run very strong, and the wind rising at the same time, makes us somewhat apprehensive for our boat, which had returned to attend D. and S. We observe them set off along the hills on foot, to walk, as we understand, to a bay called Carskey, five or six miles off, but the nearest spot at which they can hope to re-embark in this state of the weather. It now becomes very squally, and one of our jibsails splits. We are rather awkwardly divided into three parties — the pedestrians on shore, with whom we now observe Captain Wilson, mounted upon a pony — the boat with four sailors, which is stealing along inshore, unable to row, and scarce venturing to carry any sail — and we in the yacht, tossing about most exceedingly. At length we reach Carskey, a quiet-looking bay, where the boat gets into shore, and fetches off our gentlemen. After this the coast of Cantyre seems cultivated and arable, but bleak and unenclosed, like many other parts of Scotland. We then learn that we have been repeatedly in the route of two American privateers, who have made many captures in the Irish Channel, particularly at Innistruhul, at the back of Islay, and on the Lewis. They are the Peacock, of twenty-two guns, and 165 men, and a schooner of eighteen guns, called the Prince of Neuchatel. These news, added to the increasing inclemency of the weather, induce us to defer a projected visit to the coast of Galloway; and indeed it is time one of us was home on many accounts. We therefore resolve, after visiting the lighthouse at Pladda, to proceed for Greenock. About four drop anchor off Pladda, a small islet lying on the south side of Arran. Go ashore and visit the establishment. When we return on board, the wind being unfavourable for the mouth of Clyde, we resolve to weigh anchor and go into Lamlash Bay.

The Isle of Arran

7th September, 1814. — We had ample room to repent last night's resolution, for the wind, with its usual caprice, changed so soon as we had weighed anchor, blew very hard, and almost directly against us, so that we were beating up against it by short tacks, which made a most disagreeable night; as, between the noise of the wind and the sea, the clattering of the ropes and sails above, and of the moveable below, and the eternal *"ready about,"* which was repeated every ten minutes when the vessel was about to tack, with the lurch and clamour which succeeds, sleep was much out of the question. We are not now in the least sick, but want of sleep is uncomfortable, and I have no agreeable reflections to amuse waking hours, excepting the hope of again rejoining my family. About six o'clock went on deck to see Lamlash Bay, which we have at length reached after a hard struggle. The morning is fine and the wind abated, so that the coast of Arran looks extremely well. It is indented with two deep bays. That called Lamlash, being covered by an island with an entrance at either end, makes a secure roadstead. The other bay, which takes its name from Brodick Castle, a seat Duke of Hamilton, is open. The situation of the castle is very fine, among extensive plantations, laid out with perhaps too much formality, but pleasant to the eye, as the first tract of plantation we have seen for a long time. One stripe, however, with singular want of taste, runs straight up a finely rounded hill, and turning by an obtuse angle, cuts down the opposite side with equal lack of remorse. This vile habit of opposing the line of the plantation to the natural line and bearing of the ground is one of the greatest practical errors of early planters. As to the rest, the fields about Brodick, and the lowland of Arran in general, seem rich, well enclosed, and in good cultivation. Behind and around rise an amphitheatre of mountains, the principal a long ridge with fine swelling serrated tops, called Goat-Fell. Our wind now altogether dies away, while we want its assistance to get to the mouth of the Firth of Clyde, now opening between the extremity of the large and fertile Isle of Bute, and the lesser islands called the Cumbrays. The fertile coast of Ayrshire trends away to the south-westward, displaying many villages, and much appearance of beauty and cultivation. On the north eastward arises the bold and magnificent screen formed by the mountains of Argyleshire and Dumbartonshire, rising above each other in gigantic succession. About noon a favourable breath of wind enables us to enter the mouth of the Clyde, passing between the larger Cumbray and the extremity of Bute. As we advance beyond the Cumbray, and open the opposite coast, see Largs, renowned for the final defeat of the Norwegian invaders by Alexander III. [A.D. 1263]. The ground of battle was a sloping, but rather gentle, ascent from the sea, above the modern Kirk of Largs. Had Haco gained the victory, it would have opened all the south-west of Scotland to his arms. On Bute, a fine and well-improved island, we open the Marquis of Bute's house of Mount Stewart, neither apparently large nor elegant in architecture, but beautifully situated among well-grown trees, with an open and straight avenue to the seashore. The whole isle is prettily varied by the rotation of crops: and the rocky ridges of Goat-Fell and other mountains in Arran are now seen behind Bute as a background. These ridges resemble much the romantic and savage outline of the mountains of Cullin, in Skye. On the southward of Largs is Kelburn, the seat of Lord Glasgow, with extensive plantations; on the northward Skelmorlie, an ancient seat of the Montgomeries. The Firth, closed to appearance by Bute and the Cumbrays, now resembles a long irregular inland lake, bordered on the one side by the low and rich coast of Renfrewshire, studded with villages and seats, and on the other by the Highland mountains. Our breeze dies totally away, and leaves us to admire this prospect till sunset. I learn incidentally that, in the opinion of honest Captain Wilson, I have been myself the cause of all this contradictory weather. "It is all," says the Captain to Stevenson, "owing to the cave at the Isle of Egg," — from which I had abstracted a skull. Under this odium I may labour yet longer, for assuredly the weather has been doggedly unfavourable. Night quiet and serene, but dead calm — a fine contrast to the pitching, rolling, and walloping of last night.

8th September. — Waked very much in the same situation — dead calm, but the weather very serene. With much difficulty, and by the assistance of the tide, we advanced up the Firth, and passing the village of Gourock at length reached Greenock. Took an early dinner, and embarked in the steamboat for Glasgow. We took leave of our little yacht under the repeated cheers of the sailors, who had been much pleased with their erratic mode of travelling about, so different from the tedium of a regular voyage. After we reached Glasgow — a journey which we performed at the rate of about eight miles an hour, and with a smoothness of motion which probably resembles flying — we supped together and prepared to separate. — Erskine and I go tomorrow to the Advocate's at Killermont, and thence to Edinburgh. So closes my journal. But I must not omit to say that among five or six persons, some of whom were doubtless different in tastes and pursuits, there did not occur, during the close communication of more than six weeks aboard a small vessel, the slightest difference of opinion. Each seemed anxious to submit his own wishes to those of his friends. The consequence was, that by judicious arrangement all were gratified in their turn, and frequently he who made some sacrifices to the views of his companions was rewarded by some unexpected gratification calculated particularly for his own amusement. Thus ends my little excursion, in which, bating one circumstance, which must have made me miserable for the time wherever I had learned it, I have enjoyed as much pleasure as in any six weeks of my life. We had constant exertion, a succession of wild and uncommon scenery, good-humour on board, and objects of animation and interest when we went ashore—

Sed fugit interea — fugit irrevocabile tempus.